BERGSON

AN EXPOSITION AND CRITICISM

Nihil obstat

EDUARDUS MYERS,

Censor Deputatus.

Imprimatur

✠   EDM. CAN. SURMONT,

Vic : gen.

WESTMONASTERII, *die* 15 *Maii* 1913.

BERGSON

AN EXPOSITION AND CRITICISM FROM THE POINT OF VIEW OF ST. THOMAS AQUINAS

BY

THOMAS J. GERRARD

AUTHOR OF

"CORDS OF ADAM," "THE WAYFARER'S VISION,"
"THE CHURCH AND EUGENICS," ETC.

LONDON AND EDINBURGH
SANDS & COMPANY

———

ST. LOUIS, MO.
B. HERDER
17 SOUTH BROADWAY

CONTENTS

INTRODUCTION

IF we examine the various activities of the time-spirit, say in the spheres of literature, of economics, of sociology, of art, or of religion, we shall find that they may be summed up in the principle of man's self-perfectibility. Thus the chief characteristic of the time-spirit is an exaggerated subjectivism and individualism. The law of reason is set aside to make place for the predominant feeling. Sensation becomes the norm of conduct. But even healthy sensation is not of sufficient variety to provide man with constant satisfaction. When sensation has been made the leading factor in a man's life, then he soon has recourse to morbid sensation, for the sane and healthy feelings soon become exhausted. Change becomes the order of the day; nor is the question asked whether the change be for better or for worse. Anything will do provided it be a new sensation.

A new philosophy has been proposed to the world which seeks to explain and to justify these aspirations of the time-spirit. Its author is M. Henri Bergson, Professor of the Collège de France. It is a revolt against the static aspect of things. It proclaims that all is kinetics. Bergson himself calls it the philosophy of change. Indeed its great success may be set down to this consistency with itself, namely, that it provides a new sensation.

Let us not under-estimate the importance of Bergson. He has now the whole world for his audience. The small room in which he lectures in Paris is always crowded, so crowded, in fact, that many of his hearers sit through the lecture of the professor who precedes Bergson in order to ensure a place. This year he gave a course of lectures in London, but the great hall of University College was unable to accommodate one-half of those who came to hear him.* Then from October, 1913, to October, 1915, he will be Gifford Lecturer in the University of Edinburgh.

* Since then he has lectured in America.

He speaks always in French, and doubtless many of his hearers do not understand his language, whilst many more are hopelessly confused in the attempt to understand his philosophy. Nevertheless, although so many of his subtleties are hard to grasp, yet some of his main thoughts do stand out, and are making an impression on the people. It is with these that we shall concern ourselves. The custom of Catholicism is to look at books in their objective sense, that is, in the sense in which they are taken by the generality of readers. Her interest is not in the mental dexterity of the newest thinker, but in the salvation of the multitude who may be affected by him. Bergson has commanded the attention of such philosophers as Arthur James Balfour in England and William James in America. But through a host of popular writers he is gradually making his way to the people. The popular propaganda consists in a persistent repetition of conclusions rather than in a statement of reasons. Thus does the new philosophy evade the common-sense judgment of the multitude.

The following pages are offered as an attempt to place the questions at issue on a basis of common sense. And for this purpose I have deemed that there could be no better guide than that great philosopher of common sense, St Thomas Aquinas.

THOMAS J. GERRARD.

HERRENWIES,
  BADEN-BADEN,
    August, 1913.

BERGSON

CHAPTER I

GENERAL OUTLINES

THE chief works of Bergson are three. The first is *Essai sur les Données Immédiates de la Conscience*. This was written during the years 1883 to 1887, and published in 1889. It has been translated into English under the title of *Time and Free Will*. In this work the author explains one of his most fundamental concepts, namely, "duration" (*la durée*). To those who are accustomed to think in scholastic terms, the discussion may be said to be, as nearly as possible, a discussion between real and imaginary time. Real time is the actual flowing duration; whereas imaginary time is but the possible flowing duration. The imaginary time can be spread out like a map. It can either represent the intrinsic flow of real time or the extrinsic measurement of the same which we derive from the movements of the sun, moon, and stars, or by simply looking at our clocks.

In the Bergsonian method the reader is asked to put off all conventions of abstract time, and to throw himself into reality. He must *feel* the real concrete *duration*. Feeling this duration, he looks at free-will *before the act*, not after it. Thus (so he is told), although he cannot define free-will in abstract terms, yet he can establish the fact of it by observation. The scholastic reader, however, must be warned that Bergson does not mean the same thing by free-will as is meant by previous philosophers and plain men. He does not use a common coinage. He means only certain great acts of choice whereby something new is created.

The second book is *Matter and Memory (Matière et Mémoire)*. This was published in 1896. It is described as an essay on the relationship between the body and the spirit. Here the author frankly declares himself a dualist. How far he is true to his description of himself we shall see later.* The book affirms

* p. 170.

the reality of spirit and the reality of matter, and by study of the memory seeks to define the relationship between the two. It professes to avoid the difficulties of realism on the one hand, and of idealism on the other, by taking up a position midway between them. "It is a mistake to reduce matter to the perception we have of it, a mistake also to make of it a thing able to produce in us perceptions, but in itself of another nature than they. Matter, in our view, is an aggregate of 'images.' And by 'image' we mean a certain existence which is more than that which the idealist calls a *representation*, but less than that which a realist calls a *thing*— an existence placed half-way between the 'thing' and the 'representation.'"*

There is indeed a close connection between a state of consciousness and the brain, but so also is there between a coat and the nail upon which it hangs. There is, in fact, no parallelism between the psychical and the physiological processes. Memory is just the intersection of mind and matter, and particularly the memory for words. The psychical state is immensely wider than the cerebral state. The reader will

* *Matter and Memory*, p. vii.

notice in the last statement a preparation for the proposition that reason is not the only faculty by which knowledge is acquired.

These two volumes contain the ground-work upon which the third is built up, *Creative Evolution* (*L'Evolution Creatrice*). This, by far the most important of Bergson's works, was published in 1907. Here the doctrine of man's self-perfectibility is carried to its utmost possible limits. Existence, in the case of a conscious being, means nothing less than an unending process of *self-creation*. Nay, the whole universe is made up of one evolutionary flux, a self-creative process whose future is undetermined and unknown by any outside intelligence, even though it be omniscient.

Before attempting to criticise the various features of this philosophy, let us first make a general sketch of it, so that we may see how the parts hang together.

The history of the evolution of life, it tells us, shows that man's intelligence is but a department of general consciousness. It is a special faculty devised by life for a particular purpose. It is a kind of nucleus of a large nebula. It deals only with the practical ordinary affairs of life. The real glimpse at reality, which philosophy tries to get, is obtained not by the intelligence but by intuition. The intelligence, since it is created by life for one department of life, is consequently unable to see the whole of life. Even scholasticism tells us that an extended body is the connatural object of our understanding. That is why we get headaches when we occupy ourselves with abstractions for a long time without resting. Even M. Bergson has to keep using concrete examples to illustrate his metaphysical subtleties, and so also shall we have to use objects of familiar experience in order to show the bearing of scholastic principles on the new method.

In order to get a *real* knowledge of life, we must bring to the task not merely this specialised department which we call intellect, but the whole field of consciousness. We must look within ourselves, imagine ourselves in the middle of this field of consciousness, and thus *feel* the vital process. It will evade us, for it is in constant flux. But if we keep getting glimpse after glimpse of it intuitively, we shall be able to obtain the material for a theory of life and knowledge.

The intelligence can only take momentary snapshots of the things which are in motion. It makes an abstraction from the movement at a given point. Thus physical science can never comprehend reality, for it must of necessity be always behindhand. It can only touch the phenomena of life, not life itself. As far as physical science is concerned there is a corresponding re-action to every action. In her eyes there can be no free creation whatsoever. All is mechanically balanced. But philosophy can do what physical science cannot do: it can comprehend life. It touches the all-important "now," which gathers up the whole of the past and pushes forward into the future. Reality, therefore, is not something static. It is the consciousness of living. It is the intuition of life. It is, therefore, something entirely kinetic.

The intelligence breaks up this living process into states, strings them on to an imaginary string, the string being an imaginary self. Thus whilst the kinetic is the stuff which is real, the static is but an instantaneous photograph of it. When we look upon these various states as spread out in the memory, then we get an idea of imaginary Time. But when we look upon the present flux of things as the one kinetic reality, then we get the idea of real *Time*. Real time is the *fluxus ipsius nunc*, the flow of the " now " into the " now." Bergson declares it to be a continual becoming, and infers that if we try to fix it in our intelligences, we are landed at once into a static conception of it. If we would perceive its flowing nature we must *feel* it with our whole consciousness, for it is the change which we feel that is the ultimate reality.

We gather all this from looking within ourselves and perceiving the constant change. The question now arises whether that vital process which we perceive within us cannot be predicated of existence in general. The history of evolution shows that forms have succeeded forms. Types and species have come into being and have passed away, giving place to other types and species. Evolution, in a word, is a record of continuous change. The whole of life is one continuous movement like the movement of an individual man. It gathers up like a snowball all its past which it carries with it. It thrusts itself forward into the future, which it creates.

This is Bergson's opportunity to criticise, on

the one hand, the mechanical explanation of the evolutionary process, and, on the other hand, the finalist explanation. Both, he says, are weighted with the same fallacy, in that they assume that the present is contained and pre-determined in the past. Both mistake imaginary time for real time. Both take intellectual symbols for the reality instead of the active vital flux. There is nothing creative in either of them.

A further study of the history of evolution shows us two diverse lines, one the line of intelligence which has man for its ultimate stage of development, the other the line of instinct which has its perfection in ants and bees. Where instinct flourishes most intelligence flourishes least. The nature of instinct insinuates to us the nature of that faculty of direct vision which we call intuition. It is by this intuition that we are able to seize on to reality, that flux, change, duration which is so evasive to the intelligence.

Life is like a reservoir bursting forth into several streams. It is always life, but sometimes it specialises in plant forms, sometimes in animal forms, sometimes in human forms. Circumstances and opportunities modify the creative effort. In this way intelligence came into existence. Life needed it for a special purpose and so created it. The life which was identical with consciousness underwent a kind of condensation forming a luminous centre. The whole of life uses a part of itself for a special purpose. Here is the most obscure part of Bergson's philosophy. Even his most ardent disciples admit that he is far from clearly explaining himself. And obscure it must of necessity be, for, at least from our point of view, he is trying to make the intellect get behind the intellect. From his point of view he is trying to make intuition see the formation of the intellect.

The same creative evolution is also made the criterion of free-will. The question now is not, as formerly, liberty of choice between two alternative courses, but rather whether, when we act, we really create. Nay, we cannot pick out of our concrete actions those which are free and those which are not. We are only free when our action is that of our whole personality. When I have expressed myself so thoroughly as to have created something new in the world, then I have acted as a free man. Moreover, if the will only does what the intellect declares it ought to have done, it is not free. The mechanical nature of physical science precludes indeterminism. Nor is the freedom here described confined to men. It is a quality of the whole universe. Indeed it was the whole of life (which is the whole of reality) that imparted our freedom to us. All things share it in some degree.

" Life as a whole, from the initial impulsion that thrust it into the world, will appear as a wave which rises, and which is opposed by the descending movement of matter. On the greater part of its surface, at different heights, the current is converted by matter into a vortex. At one point alone it passes freely, dragging with it the obstacle which will weigh on its progress but will not stop it. At this point is humanity; it is our privileged situation. On the other hand, this rising wave is consciousness and, like all consciousness, it includes potentialities without number which interpenetrate, and to which consequently neither the category of unity nor that of multiplicity is appropriate, made as they both are for inert matter. The matter that it bears along with it, and in the interstices of which it inserts itself, alone can divide it into distinct individualities. . . . Finally consciousness is essentially free; it is freedom itself; but it cannot pass through matter without settling on it, without adapting itself to it." *

Lastly, the same necessity for free creation prevents even God from knowing the future. God Himself, indeed, is subject to the law of perpetual change. He is a kind of centre from which worlds shoot out. He is not already perfect, but rather a continuity of shooting out. Reality consists of change, and if God is real He must be for ever changing.

* *Creative Evolution*, pp. 284, 285.

CHAPTER II

THE PHILOSOPHY OF CHANGE

OBVIOUSLY the first concept that has to be dealt with in this philosophy is that which declares that reality consists in flux or change. If this philosophy be sound then we can say of nothing that it "is." Things that seem to be solid and undergo no change are but periods or cuts across the flowing. They are but snapshot views of reality, not reality itself. They belong to that imaginary time which is a symbol of space, not to the real time which is duration. A material thing endures without changing, but a living thing endures by changing. Now, asks Bergson, is the reality which is behind all appearances like a material thing that does not change? Or is it a living thing which does change? Then he answers that it must be the living stuff, namely, the ever-flowing time (*la durée*).

We turn then to St. Thomas for the corrective principle. The fallacy which Bergson makes through the whole of his treatment of change is that he does not recognise what St. Thomas calls the *ratio entitatis*. Even a thing which is in flux is a whole. There was once a baby called Woodrow Wilson. It grew and grew and grew until it became the President of the United States. But it always remained the same person, namely, Woodrow Wilson. The change from a gelatinous organism into a mighty president never destroyed its identity.

The idea of being is one of the primary observations of human experience. It is so simple and so clear to the understanding that it is incapable of further explanation. One only explains the more difficult by the more easy. But we cannot explain the one thing " being " by something else, because every something else is " being." When we say that a being is that which exists, it is almost as if we said that a book is a book and a tree is a tree. What we say about " being " then is that its nature is obvious, we see it, and we steadfastly refuse to have our intelligences muddled by pretending that we do not see it. We start with this first self-evident truth: a being is that which exists.

But a being must be some sort of being. It must be a penknife or a motor-car or an elephant or something of that kind. It must have an essence. Now an essence is that by which a thing is what it is. That by which an animal, for instance, is an animal is sensation. Sensation, therefore, is the essence of an animal. A horse has sensation, therefore a horse is an animal. A man has sensation, therefore a man is an animal. He is a higher kind of animal because of his reason, but nevertheless he is an animal. He has the essence of an animal. A full-blown being, therefore, is an essence which is actually in existence.

Now we are bound to say of an essence as such that it is unchangeable and indivisible. So long as a thing is what it is, it is what it is. A thing may change as to its integral or accidental parts, but not as to its essential parts. If its essential parts change, then the thing itself ceases to be, and something else begins to be. For instance, a pig is always a pig. When it is young it is small and thin. After twelve months of good feeding it becomes large and fat. A great change has taken place in it, but it has not changed into a baboon. In spite of all the feeding it remains a pig. The essence has remained the same. The *reality*, namely, that by which it *is* a pig, and by which it *endures* as a pig, is absolutely static.

Further, the essence is indivisible. It is true that you can have half of a carcass of a pig, but you cannot have a pig which is half pig and half aëroplane. The essence is indivisible.

The reason given by Bergson for casting aside realism is that it involves the conception of that imaginary time which is *unreal*. Reality is a flow. What does not flow is not real.

" Now, life " he says " is an evolution. We concentrate a period of this evolution in a stable view which we call a form, and when the change has become considerable enough to overcome the fortunate inertia of our perception, we say that the body has changed its form. But in reality the body is changing form at every moment; or, rather, there is no form, since form is immobile and the reality is movement. What is real is the continual change of form: the form is only a snapshot view of a transition. Therefore, here again, our perception manages to solidify into discontinuous images the fluid continuity of the real. When the successive images do not differ from each other too much, we consider them all as the waxing and waning of a single *mean* image, or as the deformation of this image in different directions. And to this mean we really allude when we speak of the *essence* of a thing, or of the thing itself." *

Incidentally, we may remark that the above description of realism is not true of the moderate realism taught by St. Thomas. The image, or shape, or form, or phenomenon, be it even the mean image, shape, form or phenomenon, is not the essence of a thing according to the doctrine of moderate realism. The essence is the abiding indivisible reality which underlies the phenomenon. It is quite true that we can only get at the thing in itself through its appearances. But the distinction is vital. It is the distinction between the *id quo* and the *id quod*. That which we see, taste, and handle is the thing, but that through which we see, taste, and handle is its appearances. We are not concerned to

* *Creative Evolution*, p. 318.

defend exaggerated realism against M. Bergson. But, on the other hand, we claim that our moderate realism provides for a permanent reality without being committed to the absurdities which are created by making reality consist in the eternal flux.

Keeping the doctrine of moderate realism in mind, we can go on to show the right use of images. They show to us the reality of space. This brings us to the converse of Bergson's radical fallacy. In making reality consist in the flux of things, he thereby thrusts out of his philosophy the concept of space. In exaggerating the time element he practically annihilates the spatial element. He puts forward *motion*, that is, change in time as the whole essence of a material thing, ignoring its length, breadth, and thickness, which (apart from all else in it) are no less its essential factors, even as change and permanency are. (Let us grant that all bodies are in a state of flux. Change, indeed, or liability to change, is of the essence of all that is material. But it is not the only factor in the essence. If it were, then we might truthfully say that all bodies are the same length, for they all consist merely of this flowing point which is " now." But no sane philosopher will go so far behind his common sense as to question the facts of common observation. Bodies are not all the same length.

There is a most luminous passage in St. Thomas which shows the unique position of the moderate realist in being able to use the good elements of idealism and realism without being caught in their fallacies. He is speaking of the intelligences of angels and disembodied spirits, and incidentally he shows how the human mind, working through the instrumentality of the brain, when once it has grasped the *idea* of a thing, can think of the thing irrespective of space and time.

" Nor again " he says " can distance in place hinder the knowledge of a disembodied soul. Distance in place ordinarily affects sense, not intellect, except incidentally, where intellect has to gather its *data* from sense. For while there is a definite law of distance according to which sensible objects affect sense, terms of intellect, as they impress the intellect, are not in *place*, but are separate from bodily matter. . . . Plainly too neither is time mingled with the intellectual activity of such beings. Terms of intellect are as independent of time as they are of place. Time follows upon local motion, and measures such things only as are in some manner placed, in space, and therefore, the understanding of a separately subsisting intelligence is above time. On the other hand, time is a condition of our intellectual activity, since we receive knowledge from phantasms that regard a fixed time. Hence to its judgments, affirmative and negative, our intelligence always appends a fixed time, *except when it understands the essence of a thing.* It understands essence by abstracting terms of understanding from the conditions of sensible things: hence in that operation it understands irrespectively of time and other conditions of sensible things." *

Here then is the precise difference between Aquinas and Bergson. Aquinas uses space as one of the data provided by sense from which the intellect may abstract matter for thought; but when once the intellect has got its idea it is able to transcend space. Bergson, being absorbed by sense, is unable to transcend space,

* *Contra Gentiles*, Lib. II., Cap. XCVI.

and consequently for the purposes of philosophy he has no alternative but to destroy it. The result is that we are shut off from the external world. We can neither derive experience from it nor enter into active communion with it. We are shut up strictly within the limits of our own subjective feelings. There being no external norm by which to correct our eccentricities, the method can lead to nothing but confusion, whether it be in truth, goodness or beauty.

We must not, however, be content with showing the unworkableness of Bergson's conclusions. We must get at the fallacy of his reasoning. This may be conveniently done, by examining his criticism of Zeno's flying arrow. By this paradox the flying arrow is motionless all the time of its flight. If it moves it occupies a number of successive positions. But it cannot occupy two successive positions unless two moments are allowed it. At any given moment, therefore, the arrow is at rest at a given point. It is, therefore, motionless at each point in its course. It is motionless, therefore, all the time it is moving.

Bergson tries to escape the paradox by denying that the arrow ever *is* at a certain point in the course.

"Yes" he says "if we suppose that the arrow can ever *be* in a point of its course. Yes again, if the arrow, which is moving, ever coincides with a position which is motionless. But the arrow never *is* in any point of its course. The most that we can say is that it might be there, in this sense, that it passes there and might stop there. It is true that if it did stop there, it would be at rest there, and at this point it is no longer movement that we should have to do with. The truth is that if the arrow leaves the point A to fall down at the point B, its movement AB is as simple, as inde-composable, in so far as it is movement, as the tension of the bow that shoots it. As the shrapnel, bursting before it falls to the ground, covers the zone with an indivisible danger, so the arrow which goes from A to B displays with a single stroke, although over a certain extent of duration, its indivisible mobility. Suppose an elastic stretched from A to B, could you divide its extension? The course of the arrow is this very extension; it is equally simple and equally un-divided. It is a simple and unique bound.

You fix a point C, in the interval passed, and say that at a certain moment the arrow was in C. If it had been there it would have stopped there, and you would no longer have had a flight from A to B, but *two* flights, one from A to C and the other from C to B, with an interval of rest. A single movement is entirely, by the hypothesis, a movement between two stops; if there are intermediate stops it is no longer a single movement. At bottom, the illusion arises from this, that the movement *once effected*, has laid along its course a motionless trajectory on which we can count as many immobilities as we will.

From this we conclude that the movement *whilst being effected*, lays at each instant beneath it a position with which it coincides. We do not see that the trajectory is created in one stroke, although a certain time is required for it; and that though we can divide at will the trajectory once created, we cannot divide its creation, which is an act in progress and not a thing. To suppose that a moving body *is* at a point of its course is to cut the course in two by a snip of the scissors at this point, and to substitute two trajectories for the single trajectory which we were first considering. It is to distinguish two successive acts where, by the hypothesis, there is only one. In short, it is to attribute to the course itself of the arrow everything that can be said of the interval that the arrow has traversed, that is to say, to admit *a priori* the absurdity that movement coincides with immobility." *

In this long and brilliant passage M. Bergson takes us into a very old philosophical dispute. It has, indeed, been called the mystery of philosophy. It were, however, a very poor consolation if, in escaping the paradox of Zeno, we must needs plunge into the absurdity of M. Bergson. Fortunately we have a distinction which rescues us from both. The question of motion harks back to that of the continuum. Nor does it make any difference whatever to the question whether the continuum is in motion or at a standstill. We could use equally well for our example either a continuous downpour of rain or a railway line. We agree wholly with M. Bergson that a local motion, namely, the transit from one place to another through a medium, is continuous and successive. Motion

* *Creative Evolution*, pp. 325-327.

must be either successive or permanent; but it cannot be permanent because then the beginning, the middle, and the end of the motion would be all one; therefore, it must be successive. It is also continuous. So far we agree.

But now comes the parting of the ways. The continuum, even though it be a kinetic continuum, a continuum in motion, such, for instance, as a flowing river, is not, as asserted by M. Bergson, indecomposable. There is a sense in which it is decomposable. The distinction by which we explain this is that proposed by Aristotle and adopted by St. Thomas—the distinction between actual parts and potential parts. The later scholastic textbooks speak of these parts respectively as formal and entitative. An actual or formal part is one that has both entity and limits. A potential or entitative part is that which has entity alone but not limits; it is, however, capable of receiving limits. When it receives them, either actually or by our imagination, then it becomes an actual or formal part.

Now we readily grant, as M. Bergson demands, that the entitative parts of a continuum have only a potential existence. That is to say, they could exist did we choose to draw the limits around them. These limits, however, are not necessary for their existence. If they were not there already we could not separate them by drawing the lines of limitation. No one gives what he has not got, so neither could a continuum give parts if it did not already have them. If you want to separate the parts of a hare so as to jug it, you must first catch your hare, together with all its parts. Nay the very idea of a continuum is that it has parts and parts, and parts outside parts. Otherwise each part would be identical with each other part. " In a continuum," says Aristotle, " there are not two halves actually but only potentially, because if they were in act they would not make a continuum." * So also St. Thomas : " In the parts of a continuum two halves of one line are potentially double in that double line which is actually one." †

With this distinction we may proceed to dissect M. Bergson's treatment of the flight of

* L. 8. phys. c. 8, 263, a. 28.

† *In partibus continui duo dimidia unius lineae duplae sunt in potentia in ipsa linea dupla quae est una actu.* In 1, 7. Met., lect. 13.

the arrow. The flight, we grant, is one undivided entity. Moreover this is true both of the moving arrow and of the motionless trajectory which it lays along its course. But the flight has potential parts, and each of which has an entity. A thing does not lose its entity because it is in movement. Nor are those potential parts any less real because their limits have not been chalked out. Of every one of those parts, even though we divide them to infinity, we can say, with unfailing judgment, that they have existed. If I make a journey in a non-stop express from New York to Washington, and the train rushes through Elizabethport, it is fooling both with ideas and with words to say that the train has never been in Elizabethport. Even though the train did not stop at the city boundaries, yet its passage through was as real as if it did stop.

So, too, is it with the arrow. Its movement is continuous and successive, but the parts of the movement have reality. Otherwise the whole movement has no reality. So, too, is it with the bursting shrapnel which is said to cover a zone with indivisible danger. If the danger were indivisible it could not do any harm to a company of men who occupied but a portion of the zone. It must destroy a whole zone full or none at all. But we know this is not true. Therefore the danger zone is divisible.

The comparison with the stretched elastic is a false analogy, for it is comparing local motion with molecular motion. Let us take the movement of each individual molecule of the elastic before and after stretching, and we shall find that its minute local motion is just as divisible and decomposable as that of the railway journey from New York to Washington.

Again, when M. Bergson says, and keeps on saying, that by the hypothesis the trajectory is created in one stroke, and that there is one movement only, then we distinguish and keep on distinguishing. One in act, we grant; one in potency, we deny.

When, however, he flourishes his ultimate reduction to absurdity and charges us with admitting *a priori*, that movement coincides with immobility, then we would remind him that we are there approaching that philosophical mystery in the presence of which it is unwise to be too dogmatic. Neither M. Bergson nor any other philosopher has solved the problem of saying exactly where the static meets the kinetic. We all know that according to theory the bouncing ball never ceases bouncing, whilst the blatant experience of our common sense tells us that it does cease bouncing. If we believe that the ball is still when we see it still, we are not absurd in doing so. Neither can we be held to be absurd for attributing reality to the various potential parts which make up the one complete movement of the arrow from A to B.

It is the exhibition of such paradoxes as the one just proposed by M. Bergson which calls forth that undying optimism of the schoolmen, confident of the reliability of common sense. It never occurred to them to ask what was reality. They might distinguish between an *ens reale* and an *ens rationis*. But the *ens* existed somewhere, either in the mind or out of it. Just as they never doubted that things were normally what they appeared to be, so they never doubted that the things which appeared to exist did exist. And that is precisely the attitude which we take up now with respect to the philosophy of change. We declare that we will not give up the use of the verb " to be." Even M. Bergson cannot get on without it. His pages bristle with it. To strike it out of our vocabulary is to plunge ourselves into the gloomiest pessimism; because if we cannot say of the things which we see and feel and think about, that they *are*, then we cannot be sure of any truth whatever.

But, suggests the Bergsonian philosopher, the use of the verb "to be" is but an artificial device for practical purposes. No, we reply, that lands us into pure pragmatism, another of the gloomy dungeons of the modern Hades. That is belied by the whole of human psychology. If I cannot be sure in my own mind that a certain statement is true, I cannot act as if it were true. And if, whilst not being sure that ideas represent the things they are supposed to represent, I go on acting as if they did represent them, then my whole life is one huge grimace.

Bergson was keen enough to note the analogous fallacy in Kant. Quite pertinently he said to him: "If we can know absolutely *nothing* of the thing in itself, how do we know that there is such a thing as a 'thing-in-itself'?" So we can thrust the same weapon through the armour of Bergson. If we *do* know the thing in itself, how can it be never itself? For if its very

essence is in a state of flux, always becoming
something, then it is never itself. If Bergson's
philosophy is right that the essences of things
are ever changing, then Kant's philosophy is
right that we know nothing of the essences
themselves. The two positions stand or fall
together.

So, too, is it with the consequences. Kant
fructified into the pessimism of Schopenhauer
and into the anarchy of Nietzsche. Bergson
must fructify into a still deeper pessimism and
more chaotic anarchy, because he promises so
much more than Kant and fulfils so much less.
Kant did make some compensation for his
critique of pure reason by undoing it with his
critique of practical reason. Report says that
M. Bergson has in preparation a book on ethics.
It is appalling to contemplate what may be the
result in conduct if the principles of the philosophy of change are rigorously applied. History
relates of another Frenchman who, a hundred
years previously, both anticipated and applied
the philosophy of change to the destiny of
nations. When Napoleon wanted an excuse for
taking Holland, he said the Alps belonged to
him; but Holland had been washed down from

the Alps; therefore Holland belonged to him. He confused, with his tongue in his cheek, the point of view of the geographer with the point of view of the physicist.

Geography tells us that countries are known according to their latitude and longitude on the earth's surface, whilst molecular physics tells us that particles of mud are known independently of their position on the earth's surface. If some Swiss mud has been carried from the source to the mouth of the Rhine, it does not follow that the essence of Switzerland has been changed into the essence of Holland. Switzerland remains up there and Holland down here, the philosophy of change notwithstanding.

In thus insisting on the value of the static element in nature, we would not wish to appear to undervalue the kinetic element. Nay, we claim that the kinetic element cannot have its full kinetic value unless it is considered in its right relation to the static. Bergson made a cardinal mistake in supposing that " being " and " becoming " were mutually exclusive. They are not. " Being " is a genus of which " becoming " is a species. Likewise " going," " desisting," " ceasing " are species of the same genus. When a thing *becomes*, it is in a *state* of becoming. The kinetic and the static elements of the process instead of being mutually exclusive are mutually complementary. If a thing could not be in a state of becoming, it could not become at all. Indeed the very reality of the flux depends upon the ultimate reality of the static concept that the flux *is*.

When the citizen of St. Louis crosses over to East St. Louis he sees the mighty Mississippi flowing beneath him. The flux is *there*. When he comes back next day all the water which he saw yesterday is gone, and another great volume has taken its place. A change has happened. But it is not the Amazon upon which he fixes his gaze. Nor is it the mere bed of the Mississippi which has remained. It is the Mississippi itself, the flowing continuum, the continuous flow of one and the same thing. Either the flux is or it is not. If it is not it has no reality. But it has reality. Therefore it is. This is our foundation. We will have our wits about us. We will turn our faces about and look this way and that, but all the time we shall sit tight on the one enduring reality, namely, that which is.

How such a radical confusion of thought could arise as to obscure this elementary dictate of common sense, we propose to show in the next chapter. It is due to the exaggerated subjectivism which under-estimates the use of the intellect, and is known as Bergson's intuitive method.

CHAPTER III

THE two most prominent ideas in the philosophy of Bergson are time and intuition. In the previous chapter we have dealt with his conception of time. We have seen that he places the very stuff of reality in this real time which is the flow of the " now," the everlasting becoming, the perpetual change. We have seen that he casts out of the realm of reality the concept of space. Space implies that bodies are side by side, that is, discontinuous, whereas real reality is continuous, an indivisible flux. We argue that such analysis of reality is fraught with metaphysical, physical, and moral absurdities.

We have suggested too that these absurdities are the outcome of a false method of philosophising, namely, Bergson's particular method of intuition. To substantiate that suggestion is the purpose of this chapter. Bergson claims that

34

the intellect is neither the supreme nor the only method of acquiring knowledge. Certain knowledge of the highest and most transcendental kind can only be obtained by a peculiar kind of intuition.

In order to find out the respective functions of intelligence and intuition, we must first look at the history of their evolution. Here, at the very threshold of the question, M. Bergson clashes with all previous evolutionists. Hitherto we have been asked to believe that from the primordial slime there was evolved first the lower forms of life, such as the amœba and the protococcus, then the higher forms of the invertebrates, then the vertebrates with some sort of a monkey as the highest but one, and finally man as a descendant from a simian ancestor.

M. Bergson now says that this is all wrong. The three orders of life, vegetative, instinctive, and rational, are not three successive stages of one and the same line of development, but rather three divergent directions of one life which split up as it grew. We hear nothing of natural selection as the cause of the different orders and species. It is the " original impetus " which does everything. The inert matter which it has to overcome serves to modify it. " The animate forms that first appeared were therefore of extreme simplicity. They were probably tiny matters of scarcely differentiated protoplasm, outwardly resembling the amœba observable to-day, but possessed of the tremendous internal push that was to raise them even to the highest forms of life. That in virtue of this push the first organisms sought to grow as much as possible, seems likely. But organised matter has a limit of expansion that is very quickly reached; beyond a certain point it divides instead of growing." *

The aptitude of matter to divide was not, however, the chief cause of the great divisions. The real causes were those which life itself bore within its bosom. We can perceive this in our own lives. We feel various incompatible tendencies all striving for expression. We choose some and abandon others. So the great initial life chooses and bifurcates. Of the many bifurcations most have become blind alleys, but two or three have become highways, one the highway of the plants, another the highway of brutes, and another the highway of man. Only

* *Creative Evolution*, p. 104.

in the last one, which leads through the vertebrates, has the passage been wide enough to
allow free movement to the full breath of life.
The chief radical difference between a vegetable
and an animal is that the vegetable manufac-
tures its own food directly from mineral sub-
stances, whilst the animal has to have the
organic food ready made. These phenomena
imply that the vegetable may remain stationary,
whilst the animal must move about in search of
food. Hence, argues M. Bergson, "the same
impetus that has led the animal to give itself
nerves and nerve centres must have ended, in
the plant, in the chlorophyllian function." *

Again, just as one great stream of life split up
into plants and animals, so the animal stream
split up into the anthropoids and the vertebrates.
In the line of the anthropoids the insect was its
culmination, whilst in the line of the vertebrates
the culmination was man. Now it so happens
that the most highly developed instinct is found
amongst the insects. Ants and bees, for
instance, have instinct much more wonderful
than that of cats or foxes. Hence M. Bergson
infers that the evolution of the animal kingdom,

* *Creative Evolntion*, p. 120.

with the exception of certain retrogressions towards vegetative life, is a bifurcation of ways, one leading to instinct, the other to intelligence.

At this point we have to institute a comparison between instinct and intelligence. In the first place they both come under the influence of the philosophy of change, inasmuch as they must be described as tendencies and not things. Just as we see plant life and animal life interpenetrating each other, so that there is no complete severance between them, so also we see instinct and intelligence interpenetrating each other. Neither lends itself to rigid definition. Nevertheless that which is instinctive in instinct is different from and opposite to that which is intelligent in intellect. What does the difference and opposition consist in?

First it may be noticed that the instruments which instinct uses are much more perfect than those which intelligence uses, but they have much less adaptability. Instinct is a faculty which uses organised implements, whereas intelligence is a faculty which uses unorganised implements. In proportion as man's implements become organised, so much the less intelligence is required in the use of them. Consider, for instance, the difference between the thought required to make a pair of shoes by hand and that to make a pair by machine. Instinct, therefore, is specialised. It uses a special instrument for a special purpose. Intelligence, however, has a much wider range. It may have clumsier tools to work with, but it can adapt them to an indefinite variety of operations. Imagine how many things a sailor can do with his pocket-knife.

This difference of instruments calls forth a difference of knowledge. If intelligence has but an unorganised instrument with which to work, it must seek out ways and means of adapting the instrument to different ends. Intelligence, therefore, is a knowledge of the relations of things. It sees the connection between subject and predicate. It makes inferences. Instinct, on the other hand, being generally unable to observe the relations of things, has a direct knowledge of the things themselves. It is a sympathy. Its direction is quite the opposite of that of intelligence. It touches life directly, whilst intelligence has only to do with inert matter. When bees are born they know their business immediately and directly. Their knowledge is perfect from the first, and independent of experience. It is this power of direct insight into life which makes instinct so much like intuition. And it is by observing the operations of instinct that we are able to put ourselves in the way of seeing things by intuition.

Before passing to the consideration of intuition itself, it will be well to give some account of the function of the intellect, for the sphere of the operations of the intellect is more familiar to us, and therefore having written this off, we shall better be able to discern the range of intuition.

The best illustration of what Bergson believes the intellect to be like is the cinematograph. The intellect does not deal with reality directly; does not touch that unceasing flow of time. It only takes snapshot views of it, and does this so constantly and readily that the snapshot views may be regarded as succeeding each other on a long cinematographical film. The intellect is only a part of the mind. It is to the mind what the eye is to the body. The body formed the eye because it needed it. So, too, the mind formed the intellect, because it wanted it for a special purpose. This purpose is to establish relations. The operation of the intellect is called forth by the needs of action.

The intellect aims, first of all, at constructing. For this purpose it uses only inert matter, and if by any chance it uses organised matter it treats it as inert. The intellect can deal only with the solid, for all else escapes it by reason of fluidity. Now for the practical purposes of life we have to take snapshots of the living flux; deal with them as having spatial quality; regard them as *provisionally final* and as so many units. It is as if we had actually taken a kodak picture of a man vaulting over a bar. We know quite well that he does not remain in mid-air, but for the practical purpose of showing our friends at home what we have seen on the athletic field, we make this static photograph. Curiously enough we are inclined to look upon the discontinuous pictures of life, which our intellect makes, as the one reality. But that is simply because such things fix our attention and rule our action. "*Of the discontinuous alone does the intellect form a clear idea.*" *

So, too, it is with regard to the objects upon which we act. We want to know whither a

* *Creative Evolution,* p. 16.

certain train is going, and whether it will stop
at our station. Its rate of progress is quite a
secondary matter. This shows that we fix our
minds on the end or meaning of the movement.
We like to have a design of it as a whole. It
is so much easier for us to plan our journey if we
have a map as well as a time-table. The intellect, therefore, is not meant to put itself into
the midst of reality for the thrill of feeling the
movement of the train; not for pure philosophy
and metaphysics, but simply for the practical
purposes of life, to show us how quickly we can
get to the city, make a fair pile of money, and
come home and gaze during the calm evening
upon clean vital becoming. The intellect deals
with the static and unchangeable simply because
it is made that way. "*Of immobility alone does
the intellect form a clear idea.*" *

By manipulating unorganised, inert, discontinuous, and immobile solids the intellect is able
to fabricate things. Indeed this is its chief
characteristic, that it has an unlimited power of
decomposing according to any law, and of
recomposing into any system.

Then, too, it has learnt the use of words.

* *Creative Evolution*, p. 164.

These, too, are mobile. They can be used first of one concrete thing, then of another, and also of ideas. Through means of language the intelligence can penetrate the inwardness of its own work. Nay, when it once sees that it can create ideas, there is no object concerning which it does not wish to have an idea. Thus it seeks to employ itself outside practical action. "There are things that intelligence alone is able to seek, but which, by itself, it will never find. These things instinct alone could find; but it will never seek them." * Intellect tries, indeed, to embrace life and thought, but it fails in its endeavour, because of its nature it seeks to have things distinct and clear, that is discontinuous; and this it cannot have because life is continuous. The "intelligible world" which the intellect makes for itself resembles the world of solids, but it is more diaphanous. The concepts are easier to deal with than images of concrete things; yet somehow they are not the perception itself of things, but the representation of the act by which the intellect is fixed on them. They are symbols, not images.

Hence logic is purely symbolic, and triumphs

* *Creative Evolution*, p. 159.

most in that science which deals with solid
bodies, namely, geometry. Whenever logic
works outside this science, so liable is it to go
wrong and miss life that it needs to be constantly
corrected by common sense. So natural is it
for intellect to look outside life, and fix itself
on inert matter, that it is sheerly an unnatural
process for it to look inward upon life and to
think that continuous real mobility, that creative
evolution which is life. *The chief negative
character of the intellect is its natural inability
to comprehend life.*

Seeing, then, that intellect gives us but a
distorted view of life, how shall we get a real
direct vision of life? The nature and the functioning of instinct suggest that it must be by
something analogous to this.

" Instinct is sympathy. If this sympathy
could extend its object and also reflect upon
itself, it would give us the key to vital
operations—just as intelligence, developed
and disciplined, guides us into matter.
For—we cannot too often repeat it—intelligence and instinct are turned in opposite directions, the former towards inert
matter, the latter towards life. Intelligence,

by means of science, which is its work, will deliver up to us more and more completely the secret of physical operations; of life it brings us, and, moreover, only claims to bring us, a translation in terms of inertia. It goes all round life, taking from outside the greatest possible number of views of it, drawing it into itself instead of entering into it. But it is to the very inwardness of life that *intuition* leads us—by intuition I mean instinct that has become disinterested, self-conscious, capable of reflecting upon its object and of enlarging it indefinitely." *

I will here make confession, and say that it took me some considerable time to see what M. Bergson meant by this new method of observing reality. I had been so accustomed to regard the intelligence as the only faculty for acquiring real knowledge, that I began to have a sinister foreboding that this new method of knowing things might have something to do with the stomach.

" Consciousness of living is the intuition of life. It is reality." I read these words over and over again, yet unable to fathom their pro-

* *Creative Evolution*, p. 186.

fundity. Then the light came to me in this wise: One night as I was in the train coming from Maldon, a man whose heart was glad with wine (or something else) turned to me and said: " I am glad I am alive, sir, aren't you? " I hesitated a moment, and then I put my hand on his shoulder and said: " You have got it." In a moment of exalted confusion he had seen the central truth of the new philosophical method.

Consciousness of living is the intuition of life. It is a psychological phenomenon which all philosophies have recognised, and which every man may observe for himself. M. Bergson's alleged discovery is not the fact itself, but the supposed enormous significance of the fact. He asks us to make a wider use of this faculty of gazing directly at life. Like the man in the Maldon train, we are too liable to be content with the first glimpse of it, to turn our backs upon it, and to seek our satisfaction in discursive reasoning. We need to wake up and see in this intuitive vision the philosophical instrument *par excellence*. By this method we can lay hold on reality itself. Kant thought that we could not touch the thing in itself because space and imaginary time were in the way. But Bergson having discarded space and the images of time, and having made real time the one reality, is able to see it by direct vision. Thus at last we have a real metaphysic, a knowledge of the *Ding-an-sich*, moving about with no *Erscheinung* to veil it from our view.

At first it might seem that this direct vision of life might give us nothing more than the elementary idea of the eternal flow of things. But that is because we have not yet made any serious effort. What, however, gives us hope is an analogous process in the world of æsthetics. The layman in art sees only the features of the objects which strike his eye. But the artist sees the intention of life, the simple movement that runs through them, binds them together, and gives them significance. " This intention is just what the artist tries to regain, in placing himself back within the object by a kind of sympathy, in breaking down by an effort of intuition the barrier that space puts between him and his model." * A sonata by Beethoven does not consist of vibrations, or melodies, or chords, nor yet in the technique of the pianist who plays, but in one undivided and indivisible whole which

* *Creative Evolution*, p. 186.

the composer saw at one glance by intuition, and which the performers, if they are to execute it properly, must see in like manner.

So also, it is suggested, must we try to see the problems of life. The intuitions of art never get further than the individual, but the intuitions of philosophy may conceivably get to universals of very rich content. But let us not expect too much. Intuition will never have so wide a range as science, nor yet will its knowledge be so definite and clear. Why? Because " intelligence remains the luminous nucleus around which instinct, even enlarged and purified into intuition, forms only a vague nebulosity." Let us take particular note of this sentence, for it explains so very much of the hazy thought of the day, and also why so many people are turning to Catholicism for something intellectual, solid, and fundamental.

Thus we have arrived at the conclusion which Bergson promised us in the beginning: Before we can have a theory of knowledge, we must first have a theory of life. The theory of life was that an initial impulse was thrust out from some centre, and that this impulse was identical with life, consciousness, time, and reality. The life thus continually flowing bifurcated, forming itself into special streams for special needs and special purposes.

In man the stream had two distinct functions to perform, namely, to deal with the objective world and with the subjective world. For these purposes it created respectively the faculties of intelligence and intuition. From these two faculties taken together, as being elements of the one consciousness, we derive our theory of knowledge. Intelligence needs the service of intuition, whilst intuition needs the service of intelligence.

" On the one hand, indeed, if intelligence is charged with matter, and instinct with life, we must squeeze them both in order to get the double essence from them; metaphysics [he means knowledge gained by intuition] is, therefore, dependent on theory of knowledge. But, on the other hand, if consciousness has thus split up into intuition and intelligence, it is because of the need it had to apply itself to matter at the same time as it had to follow the stream of life. The double form of consciousness is then due to the double form of the real, and theory of knowledge must be dependent upon metaphysics. In fact, each of these two lines of thought leads to the other; they form a circle, and there can be no other centre to the circle but the empirical study of evolution." *

We are deeply grateful to M. Bergson for this last word, for it gives us the key to the criticism we are about to make of his theory. In the formation of his theory he has depended very largely on the biological science.

We have followed with fascination his long disquisitions on the wonders of plant and animal life. But the selective principle in the choice of his examples has undoubtedly been the determination to demonstrate a continuous evolution due to intrinsic impulse. Hence such a thorough-going evolution as that of Herbert Spencer is cast aside, because it is not continuous enough. His evolution was merely an intellectual re-construction of evolution. " Such, however, is Spencer's illusion. He takes reality in its present form; he breaks it to pieces; he scatters it in fragments which he throws to the winds; then he ' integrates ' these fragments and ' dissipates their movement.'

* *Creative Evolution*, p. 188.

Having *imitated* the whole by a work of mosaic, he imagines he has retraced the design of it, and made the genesis." *   Spencer had started off to remount and redescend the course of the universal becoming, but no sooner had he started than he turned off short and gave us a picture of mosaic dispensation, formal parts side by side with formal parts, a picture whose veriest characteristic was discontinuity.

Now it so happens that the biological science has, in these latter days, given a very rude shock to all evolution which professes to be continuous.

The discoveries of Gregor Johann Mendel have come as a bolt from the blue.   Their whole tendency is to show that whatever else may be said of evolution, it cannot be said to be continuous.   The example first used in experimentation by Mendel himself shall serve to illustrate what we mean.   This example is the ordinary edible pea, *Pisum sativum*.   Taking two varieties of this, the tall and the dwarf, he cross-fertilised them.   The first generation of hybrids turned out to be all tall.   Then these hybrids in turn were sown, and the result was that both

* *Creative Evolution*, p. 385.

tall and dwarf plants grew up.   Moreover, these tall and dwarf grandchildren appeared in definite proportion, three tall specimens for every one dwarf.

Mendel experimented on 1064 plants, out of which 787 appeared as tall and 277 as dwarfs, that is three to one approximately.   To the character which remained during the three generations, namely, tall, Mendel gave the name of dominant, whilst to that which disappeared or rather remained latent in the middle generation he gave the name of recessive.

From these experiments two laws are deduced.   The first is that when two races possessing two antagonistic peculiarities are crossed, the hybrid exhibits only one, and as regards this character the hybrid is undistinguishable from its parent.   The second is that in the formation of pollen or egg-cell, the two antagonistic peculiarities are segregated, so that each ripe germ-cell carries either the one or the other of these peculiarities, but not both.   Thus the laws positively exclude any intermediate conditions.   Discontinuity, therefore, is of their very essence.   Further, what is true of inheritance is also true of variation.   Professor Bateson, the apostle of Mendelism in England, does speak of continuous and discontinuous variation. But of the continuous variations he says that they are very slight, in fact almost insensible, differences of size, colour, etc., in a series of individuals having the same parent. But these fluctuate about a given mean. They never shade off into other forms. Thus where continuity does appear, it would seem only to accentuate the fact of discontinuity. And when the discontinuity affects both inheritance and variation, there is a double reason for doubting a continuous evolution.

We are quite aware that Mendel's laws are not universally accepted in the scientific world. Nor have they, owing to the complexity of interfering circumstances, been widely verified in the qualities of the human species. But they have assumed an importance so great in the scientific world, and have received such marvelous confirmation by the experiments of De Vries, Bateson, and Biffen, as to throw the gravest possible doubt on that theory of life from which M. Bergson develops his theory of knowledge. The chief note of Bergson is continuity, whereas the chief note of Mendel is discontinuity. I

have searched in vain through the works of
M. Bergson for some reference to the theory
of Mendel.

What is made doubtful by a study of biology
is made more than doubtful by a study of
psychology. With regard to this theory of life,
which M. Bergson takes as his foundation, we
may ask what does he mean by life? He tells
us: " Existence in time is life." Once again he
changes the current coinage. It is quite true
that we now speak of the life of a motor-car,
and when a medical practitioner is calculating
whether motor-cars or horses are the more
economical, he considers their lives on the Bergsonian principle of existence in time. Which
will last the longer and which will cost the less?
But, according to the current use of words and
ideas, the life of a motor-car is but metaphorical
life when compared with the life of a horse.
The chauffeur needs no whip because the motor-
car has no feelings and no consciousness. Such
a kind of life then can be no prerequisite for a
theory of knowledge. On the contrary there is
required a theory of knowledge before the
motor-car can have any life at all, metaphorical
or otherwise. The construction of a motor-

car is wholly the outcome of mechanical science.

Next we must eliminate from the question the life of plants. We may readily grant that there are borderland specimens of plants showing signs of sensation. But taking the whole vast order of the vegetable world, we have to say of it that it has no sensation and no consciousness. An oak tree does not squeak or kick if you stick pins into it. That stream of life, therefore, which is purely vegetable has no exigency and tendency to concentrate for itself a nucleus of intelligence. The vegetable life is no prerequisite for a theory of knowledge.

The question is thus narrowed down to one of feeling and intelligence. But here M. Bergson unfortunately uses words of double or vague meaning. For instance, he uses the word "mind" as including instinct and intelligence, whereas hitherto mind has always been taken to exclude instinct or feeling. So also he speaks of intuition as instinct that has become self-conscious and capable of reflecting on its object, whereas at other times he speaks of it as the power of direct vision.

Now a faculty cannot be sense and intelli-

gence at the same time, because these two faculties, whether we regard them as things or as
tendencies, are essentially distinct. Neither
can a faculty act directly and reflexly at the same
time. If, however, M. Bergson means that
intuition can act first directly and then reflexly,
then so far he is intelligible. We understand,
but we do not agree with him.

As we have already remarked, the most ardent
students of M. Bergson complain of his obscurity
concerning the borderland of intelligence and
intuition.

We must try, therefore, to disentangle the
matter for him. We must insist on the essential distinction between intellect and sense.
Imagination is sense, and instinct is sense
because both pertain directly to the organic
faculty. The intellect undoubtedly depends
upon them for material wherewith to think.

But the consciousness of comparative and
judicial acts, together with the consciousness of
universal and abstract concepts, proves conclu-
sively that we have a suprasensuous faculty. If
I see a horse and a cow I can not only enjoy the
sight of them, but I can make comparisons,
observe how far they are like or unlike each

other. So, too, I can pass from this or that horse in particular to the concept "horse" in general. Consequently we must have some power, distinct from sense, by which we do these things. That power we call intellect.

With this distinction we may examine M. Bergson's picture of consciousness: "Intelligence is the luminous nucleus around which instinct, even enlarged and purified into intuition, forms only a vague nebulosity." That part of consciousness, therefore, which is not intelligence is instinct or intuition. Instinct and intuition, therefore, must be sensation. And this is what M. Bergson repeats over and over again. We are to set our intelligence aside, because that deals only with solids and the representations of reality, and we are to put ourselves into the eternal flux and *feel* the reality of it. That consciousness of living, therefore, which is the dawning of a new philosophy, according to M. Bergson, has been rightly named in the scholastic system as the *sensus intimus*, and rightly defined as the faculty by which we recognise as our own the various modifications of our senses.

This was the sense which had just functioned

in the man in the Maldon train. Then his intellect reflected upon it, and the reflection caused him the joy which he so ardently wished to share with me. Moreover, this explanation of intuition as a feeling is the one which has been generally taken by those who have tried to put M. Bergson's doctrine to a practical application.

When asked for reasons for certain views, they reply that they have arrived at their conclusions by another way than that of reason. They have seen the truth intuitively. They *feel* that it must be true, and therefore it *is* true. And this is just where the danger of M. Bergson's doctrine comes in.

Naturally such an exaggeration of feeling would require a corresponding debasement of reason. This, therefore, shall be our next point, to examine the various limits which have been set to reason by M. Bergson.

Our first objection is to the statement that it is of the discontinuous alone that the intellect forms a clear idea. There is a fallacy here which is due to the confusing of imagination with intelligence. When we try to imagine an object in motion, especially if the motion be rapid, the phantasm appears to us as somewhat blurred. The internal sense of the imagination is very similar to the external sense of eyesight. The eye requires time to adjust itself to rapid motion, and if this time is not allowed, the moving object appears as fogged. If I tie a piece of wood to the end of a string and whiz it round, the wood will appear as a circle.

The Futurist painters * made exactly the same fallacy when they tried to express movement through means of paint on canvas. Thus if they wanted to paint a man in the act of swimming they painted two men and smudged one into the other. Pictorial representation, whether on a photographic film or on a painter's canvas, or on the retine of the eye, or on the substance of the brain, requires time and space, requires to be discontinuous, if it is to be clear. But not so with intellectual representation.

The intellect, whilst using time and space as its handmaids, is able to transcend them. I can conceive of local motion even apart from the object which is moving. I can conceive of life even apart from the animal which lives. The fallacy which is here committed by M. Bergson

* See article in the *Dublin Review*, July, 1912.

is that known as the illicit transit from the ontological to the logical order. He mixes up
sensitive phantasy with intellectual thought.

So also is it with the statement, that of immobility alone does the intellect form a clear idea.
This statement is connected with the previous
one by the doctrine that motion is continuous
and indivisible, a doctrine which we disproved in
our first chapter. Without, however, referring to
that doctrine or its refutation, we can say directly
that the intellect can get a clear idea of mobility.
I can compare, for instance, mobility with
immobility, and I can recognise precisely,
distinctly, and clearly that there is as much
difference between them as there is between
chalk and cheese. It is the imagination that
renders the immobile clearly and the mobile con-
fusedly. The intellect can have clear conceptions of both. Once again, M. Bergson has
been the victim of the illicit transit, mistaking
that which is spiritual for that which is
material.

With what M. Bergson says of the intellect's
unlimited power of decomposing ideas according
to any law and of recomposing them into any
system, we cordially agree. In our language

we call it division and composition. Here we come to the point where intellect meets intuition.

We object to the statement that the chief negative character of the intellect is its natural inability to comprehend life.

First, M. Bergson misrepresents the power of the intellect when he says that its concepts are not the perception itself of things. He wanders still further from the truth when he says that these conceptions are something less than images, and are, in fact, merely symbols. He falls into an error somewhat similar to that of Kant. Kant said that the intellect could know nothing of the things in themselves, but only of their appearances. Bergson says that intuition alone sees the things in themselves. The intellect does not. The intellect sees only symbols of the things, and symbols, moreover, which are not images. That means that our intellectual concepts have so little correspondence with the things they represent that they are not even natural symbols of them, but merely conventional symbols.

The refutation of this doctrine is the same as the refutation of that of Kant. It is an appeal to common sense and to the universal judgment of mankind. When I put my teeth into a rosy apple, can I be quite sure that it really is an apple, and that it is not possibly a cricket ball, which is the conventional symbol for an apple? When I am talking to President Wilson can I be quite sure that it really is Mr Wilson, and not possibly Mrs Eddy, who may be the conventional symbol for Mr Wilson.

No, we decline to be moved from that mediæval scholastic intuition which is the common sense of all nations, always and every-where, the *semper*, *ubique et ab omnibus* all taken together, namely, that things are normally what they appear to be, and not merely conventional symbols of the same.

Hence although we do not go so far as to say that the intellect is naturally able to comprehend life, yet we do go so far as to say that it is as naturally able to comprehend life as it is to comprehend the solid objects of the external world or anything else at all. The intellect does not comprehend things in the sense that it knows everything that can possibly be known about them. But it does comprehend them in the sense that it knows their essence, namely that by which they are what they are. And to this kind of comprehension life is no exception.

The intellect has no difficulty whatever in formulating its definition of life—the activity by which a being moves itself. And when asked for further explanation it has no difficulty in saying that the word " move " includes all forms of change or alteration, and includes the energies of feeling, intelligence, and will, as well as local motion; and that the word " activity " is understood as having an immanent character as opposed to transient, that is, beginning and ending as an internal principle.

All this belittling of intelligence, however, is but the natural result of M. Bergson's theory of life. In trying to make intuition a continuation of instinct he got on to the wrong line. Intuition is a mental faculty, whereas he tried to make it a sensitive faculty. He did not recognise that there are organic internal senses as well as organic external senses. And being on the line of organic internal sense, he came to that operation of it by which it feels the present state of the body, the flow of the now, and thereupon called it intuition. Then, instead of regarding this organic sense as ministrant to intellect, he dragged in the reflections which the intellect made upon it, and called those reflections the reflections of the intuitive faculty.

Bergson is quite clear on the point. " But it is to the very inwardness of life that intuition leads us." * So far he has observed the operation of the organic sense. Then he continues: " By intuition I mean instinct that has become disinterested, self-conscious, capable of reflecting upon its object and enlarging it indefinitely." † There he adds on to the sensation the reflective function of the intelligence, but retains all under the same name of intuition. He observes that the primary sensation has a natural tendency to lend itself to the intellect to be reflected upon. But he asks us to resist this natural tendency and drive on this so-called intuition to explore the deeper experiences of life. Instead of using his intelligence to abstract essences from life, man must plunge into the stream and *feel* life.

Unfortunately there is one great obstacle to this method, and that is the great fact of space. Therefore, according to Bergson, space must be annihilated. Thus we have arrived at the con-

* *Creative Evolution*, p. 186.
† *Ibid.*, p. 186.

clusion which we proposed at the end of our last chapter. The discarding of space and the placing of reality in the flow of time was due to this exaggerated subjectivism which substitutes feeling for intelligence, and which under the false title of mental intuition sets up sensation as the philosophical faculty.

But it may be asked: is it not true that artists have visions of great conceptions? Is it not true that great politicians conceive vast policies *intuitively*? It is not true that great generals seize upon great strategies *instinctively*? Is it not true that great Saints and Doctors of the Church have a tremendous grasp of huge fields of doctrine, and see many truths so swiftly that it can hardly be ascribed to discursive reasoning? It is.

But the insight is not due to that organic sensation which announces to us our subjective feelings at the present passing moment. Nor is it due to that stultification of the intellect which confines its powers to the limits of space and imaginary time. Nor yet again is it due to an aimless guessing at conclusions merely because we would like them to be true or feel them to be true. No, there is a sane doctrine

E

of intuition and a sane doctrine of mental instinct.

We propose to sketch this in our next chapter, which will take the form of a comparison between Bergson, Newman, and Aquinas.

CHAPTER IV

BERGSON, NEWMAN, AND AQUINAS

THERE can be no doubt that M. Bergson has hit upon certain facts of experience which are of enormous importance in the formation of a philosophy. Amongst these may be cited the fact of our last and ultimate phase of consciousness, that which we experience at the living, present moment; the fact of the interpenetration of feelings with feelings, of ideas with ideas, of feelings with ideas; the fact of the organic connection between thought and the other activities of life.

Because these facts are so important we shall not be content with merely criticising his interpretation of them, but we shall offer, step by step, an interpretation of our own. The merely destructive critic is of some use, but not much. If we pull down we ought also to build up. Our architects for the present plan are Newman and Aquinas.

First, there comes intuition, strictly so-called. That is an operation of the mind, not of an organic sense. It is defined as an act by which the intellect perceives a truth immediately evident. For instance, it is immediately evident to me that I am not you and you are not I. To bring any intermediate evidence to prove it would be to act as a fool. The truth is self-evident. Being certain of my own identity, I can pass out of myself and consider a number of other truths in the outside world also self-evident. For instance, " The whole is greater than its part." And again: " Good must be done and evil avoided." Concerning intuitions of this kind there is no practical difficulty.

But as we get deeper and deeper into the processes of thought, we find that there are truths which, while self-evident to some minds, require discursive reasoning for others. Minds made the more capable by nature or by culture can see complex truths more readily than minds not so capable. God, having a perfect all-comprehensive mind, sees everything at one intuitive glance, *per unam speciem*.

The question before us is this: Has man a faculty by which he can see complex truths at a glance? Can he arrive at truths not generally self-evident without passing through the process of discursive reasoning? Can he come to a sublime concept by any faculty such as instinct or intuition and apart from the faculty of reason?

Here there is need of several distinctions. Our first distinction shall be that of the word "instinct." By instinct, considered as a function of organic sense, man cannot arrive at even the simplest abstract truths. Much less, therefore, can he arrive at the more complex truths by instinct.

Instinct considered as an organic faculty can only touch single concrete objects. It is by its very nature utterly incapable of making the slightest reflection. It is common to both brutes and men, but brutes possess it in a much more perfect degree than men.

Cardinal Newman has a very pregnant paragraph, in which he shows that the principle of the objectivity of thought (*I not you and you not I*), the first of our first principles, is founded on the animal instinct, yet is essentially distinct from it. He says:

"Next, as to the proposition that there

are things existing external to ourselves, this
I do consider a first principle, and one of
universal reception. It is founded on an
instinct; I so call it, because the brute
creation possesses it. This instinct is
directed towards individual phenomena, one
by one, and has nothing of the character of
a generalisation; and, since it exists in
brutes, the gift of reason is not a condition
of its existence, and it may justly be considered an instinct in man also. What the
human mind does is what the brutes cannot
do, viz., to draw from our ever recurring
experiences of its testimony in particulars
a general proposition, and, because this
instinct or intuition acts whenever the
phenomena of sense present themselves, to
lay down in broad terms, by an inductive
process, the great aphorism, that there is an
external world, and that all the phenomena
of sense proceed from it. This general
proposition, to which we go on to assent,
goes (*extensivè*, though not *intensivè*) far
beyond our experience, illimitable as that
experience may be, and represents a
notion." *

Here Newman sheds light which reveals to

* *Grammar of Assent*, pp. 61-62.

us at once the confusion of Bergson's thought. For Newman shows exactly where instinct ends and where intellect begins. Instinct provides intellect with material to work upon. Instinct is not, as Bergson says, disinterested, self-conscious, capable of reflecting upon its object and enlarging it indefinitely. On the contrary, instinct presents sensible images from which intellect makes abstractions.

Bergson's great mistake was in making intellect and instinct act in opposite directions, and in giving them entirely different fields of action. They act in the same direction, but each in a different manner. They both have the same things for their objects, but under different aspects. Sense has for its object the appearances of a thing, whilst intellect has for its object the thing itself, and not the appearance of it.

We will inevitably land in confusion if we do not rid ourselves of the notion that instinct and intellect act at variance, and in opposition to each other. While each has its distinct sphere, both act in harmony with each other, instinct spontaneously ministering to intellect.

St. Thomas is perhaps more generous than

Newman in admitting similarities between animal instinct and human intelligence. He goes so far as to use the word " intellect " for some of the higher operations of animal instinct. But he is careful to qualify the word by calling it " passive " (*intellectus passivus*), and by insisting on its singular, sensitive, organic nature. He also calls it the *vis cogitativa*. He shows that this is not the differentiating faculty between brutes and man, but that man has a real intellect, the *intellectus possibilis*, so called because of its unlimited power to think all possible ideas. St. Thomas says:

"An incident of the sensitive part cannot constitute a being in a higher kind of life than that of the sensitive part, as an incident of the vegetative soul does not place a being in a higher kind of life than the vegetative life. But it is certain that phantasy and the faculties consequent thereon, as memory and the life, are incidents of the sensitive part. Therefore, by the aforesaid faculties, or by any one of them, an animal cannot be placed in any higher rank of life than that which goes with the sentient soul. But man is in a higher rank of life than that. Therefore the man does not live the life that is proper to him by virtue of the aforesaid ' cogitative faculty ' or ' passive intellect.' " *

And again:

" Sense is found in all animals, but animals other than man have no intellect: which is proved by this, that they do not work like intellectual agents, in diverse and opposite ways, but just as nature moves them to fixed and uniform specific activities, as every swallow builds its nest in the same way. . . . *No sense has reflex knowledge of itself and its own activity*: the sight does not see itself nor see that it sees. But intellect is cognisant of itself, and knows that it understands." †

This essential distinction between sense and intellect obliges us to recognise that a man can no more think with his instinct than he can with his big toe. The right functioning of instinct is a necessary condition of clear thinking, just as is the right functioning of blood circulation at our lower extremities. We cannot study

* *Contra Gentes*, Lib. II., Cap. LX.
† *Ibid.*, Lib. II., Cap. LXVI.

metaphysics if we are distracted with gout. But
no amount of vegetative operation or keen
instinct can see reflexive truth.

Having made quite clear the distinction
between instinct and intelligence, properly so-
called, we may pass on to consider those higher
acts of the mind in which the mind seems to act
just as instinct does, and in which it seems to go
directly to its object, complex though it be,
without appearing to pass through the intermediate stages of discursive reasoning.

First, however, let us admit that the operations of some particular minds would seem to
give a handle to that part of Bergson's philosophy which limits the operations of intellect to
space, and to explicit processes analogous to the
cinematograph.

There are people with what we call rigid
minds and wooden dispositions. St. Thomas
the Apostle was one. My distinguished friend,
Dr Adrian Fortescue, is another. As he passes
from the major to the minor of an argument,
you can almost hear the click, and when he
passes from the minor to the conclusion, the
click becomes a snap. He is perfectly at home
with such a theme as the Orthodox Eastern

Church, because that Church has been petrified for nearly nine centuries. But if he writes a book on such a vital thing as the Roman Liturgy, it is only to chronicle what has been said about it by others.

Of course, the angelic Doctor had taken stock of this sort of mind, for doubtless there were such amongst the *savants* of Paris in his day even as in Bergson's. He says:

> " There are some who do not accept that which is said to them unless it be said in a mathematical way. And this happens on account of the custom of those who have been brought up on mathematics, for custom is a second nature. This also can happen to some people on account of their indisposition, to those, namely, who have a strong imagination and a not very elevated understanding."

Nor is this quoted as in any way disparaging to the class. They have their fitting place in the general scheme of things. They make the bricks of which the builder constructs the edifice.

Wherefore, since these things are so, we may

proceed with our construction. We may observe next that there is a principle in the philosophy of St. Thomas which does account for that interpenetration of the faculties of which M. Bergson makes so much. This is known as the principle of dichotomy.

It asserts that man is a composite being of two principles, and of two only, namely, body and soul. There are not two souls or two forms. It is the same soul in man which thinks, wills, feels, vegetates, and actuates the primary matter. If, therefore, all these operations are but the activities of one and the same spiritual substance, namely, the soul, they must work in mutual harmony. They must have something more than an artificial communication with each other. They must have an organic connection with each other. But at the same time each one must perform the work which it was made to perform, each one must act according to its own nature. The will must not be expected to circulate the blood, neither must the sensitive faculty be expected to do the thinking. Each must do its own proper work. To emphasise this important point we print the formula in capitals: SECUNDUM NATURAM PRO-

PRIAM (*according to its proper nature*): that by keeping this phrase prominently before us we may secure our reasoning process from degenerating into Bergsonian confusion.

Bergson professed to bring in the whole man as the total principle which searched for truth, but by confusing mind and sense, and by casting out the spatial relationship, his whole man became the whole man minus intelligence, while our whole man retains all his faculties. They act organically. Neither sensation nor volition usurps the office of intelligence. All the functions and faculties act in harmony with each other, but each according to its own nature, *secundum naturam propriam.*

St. Thomas thus describes the interaction of the various powers:

> " According to the order of nature, on account of the combination of the forces of the soul in one essence, and of the soul and body in one composite being, the superior forces, and also the body, influence each other, and hence it is from the soul's apprehension that the body is transmuted . . . and likewise conversely the transmutation of the body re-acts upon the soul. Simi-

larly the higher powers act upon the lower powers, as when passion in the sensual appetite follows upon an intense movement of the will, or when close study restrains and hinders the animal powers from their acts; and conversely when the lower powers act upon the higher powers, and from the vehemence of the passions in the sensual appetite the reason is darkened." *

Owing to this basic and organic connection between the faculties and functions, the mind is able to make rapid and spontaneous acts, which, in the concrete, we find difficult to analyse. It makes quick and spontaneous abstractions. Then in the same quick way it can pass from one concrete truth to another without having any explicit attention fixed on the intermediate universal term by which it does so. Thus I can say: "John Smith is a man, therefore he can make mistakes." "John Smith is a man," that is one concrete truth. "He can make mistakes," that is another concrete truth. The universal middle term by which I pass from one to the other is: "It is human to err." This middle term is not expressed, but it is implied.

* *Quest. disp. de Veritat.* qu. 26, a. 10.

Afterwards, when we are talking about our quick mental processes, we can see that the intellect has not gone out of its province, nor has it drawn any other faculties into its province. Why? Because each faculty and function has acted according to its own nature.

Further, when the intellect has had much practice in thinking, it forms intellectual habits. By these habits it can pass more rapidly still from one truth to another. Nay, it can even summarise long intellectual processes. Hence we have a recognised form of syllogism, called the enthymeme, in which a premise is left out, because it can be perceived implicitly. This is why the writings of great thinkers are so frequently difficult to understand. A well-trained mind is able to suppress, or rather to imply, much intermediate reasoning which a less trained mind would have to render explicitly.

Now for this quick process of thought three kinds of mental habits are needed. First there is required the habit of common sense. That is the faculty of seeing those truths easily which the average mind sees easily. In other words, a man must not be a stupid. He must have the ordinary capacity for seeing such truths as " twice two are four," and that " parallel lines will never meet." This mental habit is called *understanding*.

Then there is required the habit of combining these first principles. By constant practice a man can acquire a facility in combining simple ideas, dividing complex ideas, and re-combining the elements of certain complex truths to make up certain other complex truths. When this facility has been acquired the man passes easily from the known to the unknown. Eventually many of his conclusions, which previously needed to be worked out laboriously, become to him self-evident. The habit by which he does this is called the habit of *science*.

Hence a physical scientist can see at a glance that water is a combination of oxygen and hydrogen. A moral scientist can see at a glance that marriage is the foundation of society. Thus a proposition which needs discursive reasoning for the average mind may be intuitive for a mind skilled in that particular science or branch of knowledge.

Thirdly, there is a mental habit which enables a man to handle the principles and conclusions of a science easily. This is a further extension of the power of composition and division; the power to study the various sciences, to trace them back to their ultimate sources, and to ordain them to man's highest happiness and well-being, that is called the habit of *wisdom*. This faculty, too, like those of science and understanding, can be so trained as to act rapidly, easily, and spontaneously. And when it can do this perfectly, then its operation is of the nature of an intuition.

In the whole of the above process, from the simplest dictates of common sense up to the highest acts of expert wisdom, one thing is abundantly clear, namely, that the operation of the intellect is never a blind operation. It is one of vision from beginning to end, a vision of evidence.

First there is the vision of first principles, the sight of those primary truths which we liken to the vision of the bodily eye. "It is plain as a pike-staff," we say. Then there is the vision of science, a vision of inferences based upon experiment. Finally there is the vision of wisdom, that grasp of a large situation which appears in its highest perfection in men of

F

genius, in great generals, great statesmen, great poets, great artists. Thus by a synthesis, based upon the Aristotelian theory of habits, does St. Thomas build up his theory of intellectual vision.

By a different method Cardinal Newman arrives at almost the same conclusion. His method is the analytic and comparative. He takes the phenomena of assent in different spheres of inquiry, he observes that men actually arrive at certitude in law, in politics, in war, etc., and argues that they can arrive at certitude in the same way as regards speculative and religious truth.

Just as St. Thomas uses the term " passive intellect " to describe something which is merely organic sense, so Newman uses the word " sense " to describe something which is strictly intellectual.

That spontaneous act by which a man sums up all available evidence and assents to a conclusion which is the result of it, Newman calls an operation of the illative sense. It is exactly the same operation which St. Thomas calls an act of wisdom, except that whereas St. Thomas extends its range to both practical and speculative truth, Newman limits it to speculative truth alone.

That Newman and Aquinas, approaching the question from such opposite points of view, should be in such perfect harmony with each other is explained by the fact that they both possessed the same identical key. This was the Greek word *phronesis*—that final judgment which is so spontaneous, natural, and quick that it may be likened to the spontaneity and quickness of instinct, and may be called, in its perfection, the power of intuition. And the Greek word which represents its foundation may be taken for an everlasting sign that the operation is strictly intellectual, and not a re-action of the organic sense.

Says St. Thomas:

> " The power of intellect first of all apprehends something, and this act is called 'understanding'; secondly, however, it takes that which it apprehends, and orders it towards knowing or doing something else, and this is called 'intention'; whilst, however, it is engaged in the inquiry of that which it intends, it is called 'excogitation'; but when it examines that which it

has thought out with other certain truths, it is said to know or to be wise. And this is the function of *phronesis*, or *sapientia*; for it is the function of wisdom to judge." *

Newman writes:

" This power of judging and concluding, when in its perfection, I call the illative sense, and I shall best illustrate it by referring to parallel faculties, which we commonly recognise without difficulty. . . . As regards moral duty, the subject is fully considered in the well-known ethical treatises of Aristotle. He calls the faculty which guides the mind in matters of conduct by the name of *phronesis*, or judgment. This is the directing, controlling, and determining principle in such matters, personal and social. What it is to be virtuous; how we are to gain the just idea and standard of virtue; how we are to approximate in practice to our own standard, what is right and wrong in a particular case, for the answers in fullness and accuracy to these and similar questions the philosopher refers us to no code of laws, to no moral treatise,

* *Summa*, p. I., qu. 79, a. 10, ad 3m.

because no science of life, applicable to the case of an individual has been or can be written. Such is Aristotle's doctrine, and it is undoubtedly true. An ethical system may supply laws, general rules, guiding principles, a number of examples, suggestions, landmarks, limitations, cautions, distinctions, solutions of critical or anxious difficulties; but who is to apply them to a particular case? whither can we go, except to the living intellect, our own, or another's?"*

These quotations have an additional value when we remember that Newman was not familiar with the works of Aquinas.† I am also of the opinion that Newman had not read Aristotle's *Metaphysics*, else why should he draw his parallel from the *Nicomachean Ethics*, when the idea he wanted was there to his hand in the *Metaphysics* and already applied to his purpose. It was a happy fault on his part, if fault it was. for it shows us at once the independence and the

* *Grammar of Assent*, pp. 353 and 354.

† He knew his way about them, so to speak, but we shall search him in vain for evidence of knowledge of St. Thomas.

harmony of the three great minds, Newman, Aquinas, and Aristotle.

It is to St. Thomas rather that we must look for the more complete synthesis. He has one *phronesis* overruling the totality of man's life, whereas Newman asks for a *phronesis* for each faculty. Once again we find St. Thomas absolutely abreast of modern times.

We may now examine the difference between the doctrine of Bergson and that of Newman and Aquinas. The higher intuition of Bergson is purely organic and sensitive, unintellectual, acting only in response to its proper object. The higher intuition and instinct of Newman and Aquinas is strictly intellectual, but nevertheless spontaneous, quick and easy, when in its perfection, and only called sense or instinct by reason of a certain analogy which it bears to them.

He, therefore, who uses the intuitive method of Newman and Aquinas must use his intellect to the utmost of its capacity. All its discursive reasoning is gathered up in the form of habit, and is summarised for the service of that last ultimate judgment which comes as an intuition. Thus the intuition, instead of being a blind piece of guess-work, is the total result of the whole of the man's thought. It is an illation characterised by the highest wisdom.

On the contrary, in the Bergsonian method, the seeker after truth begins by maiming his intellect. He is like a man who would dig a hole, and begins by smashing his spade. Intuition and intellect are declared to work in opposite directions, the one aiming at life, the other at inert matter. Intuition, according to Bergson, is not a special perfection of the intelligence, but a special perfection of animal instinct.

The doctrine of Newman and Aquinas has all the advantages which Bergson is striving for, but which he fails to obtain. Both Newman and Aquinas are fully in touch with life. Aquinas begins with the living *ego*. Then from the *ego* he communicates with the outside world and receives impressions. These impressions modify the *ego*, and become the material upon which the mind works. Hence the axiom found throughout the whole system of St. Thomas, that nothing is in the intellect except what has previously been in the senses.

Then, when the mind has obtained the

material with which to work, there goes on a constant kinetic process. Thought is as much a present necessity for the mind as air is for the lungs. Hence the composition and division of ideas goes on in one constant flow. First principles are worked up into knowledge and knowledge into wisdom. Wisdom being that vital mobile faculty of the mind by which it peers into truth and forms its explications and applications. St. Thomas, however, takes this so much for granted that it seems hardly worth while for him to emphasise it.

Newman, on the contrary, is never tired of insisting on the need of associating thought with life, or rather of looking upon thought as a form of life. Whilst ever insisting on the intellectual nature of the illative sense, he deprecates too much introspection and self-analysis. " Introspection of our intellectual operations is not the best means of preserving us from intellectual hesitations. To meddle with the springs of thought and action is really to weaken them." *

Hence it is well to let the mind act naturally. not to force one element towards the abstract flow of life and another to the solids of the out-

* *Grammar of Assent*, pp. 216 and 217.

side world; not to confine reflection to subjective experience derived from subjective experience, but to use a subjective experience which is constantly refreshed from the objective world.

> "Instinctively, even though unconsciously, we are ever instituting comparisons between the manifold phenomena of the external world as we meet them, criticising, referring to a standard, collecting, analysing them. . . . We apprehend spontaneously, even before we set about apprehending, that man is like man, yet unlike; and unlike a horse, a tree, a mountain, or a monument, yet in some, though not the same respects, like each of them. And in consequence, as I have said, we are ever grouping and discriminating, measuring and sounding, framing cross classes and cross divisions, and thereby rising from particulars to generals, that is from images to notions." *

Thus Newman is in complete harmony with the scholastics. Bearing this fundamental harmony in mind we can go the whole way with him when he shows us his method as a vital

* *Grammar of Assent*, p. 30.

process. We know now what he means when he says: "Logic makes but a sorry rhetoric with the multitude; first shoot round corners, and you may not despair of converting by a syllogism." *

And again: "It is the mind that reasons or assents, not a diagram on paper." † The mind acts according to its own nature, that is, it normally keeps the laws of the syllogism, even though, through rapidity of action, it does not reflect on them. "It is to the living mind that we must look for the means of using correctly principles of whatever kind, facts or doctrines, experiences or testimonies, true or probable, and of discerning what conclusion from these is necessary, suitable, or expedient, when they are taken for granted; and this, either by means of a natural gift, or from mental formation and practice, and a long familiarity with those various starting-points." ‡

St. Thomas crowns his doctrine by showing how it is directed to man's eternal interests through the special gifts of the Holy Spirit. In

---

* *Grammar of Assent*, p. 94.
† *Ibid.*, p. 180.
‡ *Ibid.*, p. 360.

the natural order man orders his life aright by making a fair equipoise between external evidence and subjective appreciation of the same. He does not shut himself up within himself, depending entirely on his own power of self-perfectibility. He acknowledges that he is a social animal, and depends very largely for his due perfection on the experience and influence of his fellow-beings.

But if self-perfectibility is a crude fallacy in the natural order, much more so is it in the supernatural order where man is destined to a life so much beyond his natural powers. Wherefore St. Thomas works into his system the revealed truth concerning the gifts of the Holy Spirit. Corresponding with the three habits of mind by which man passes from first principles to highest intuition, there are the three divine gifts of understanding, knowledge, and wisdom (*intellectus, scientia, sapientia*).

" Thus, therefore, concerning the truths which are proposed to be believed on faith, two things are required on our part. First, they must be penetrated and grasped by the intellect; and this pertains to the gift of understanding. Secondly, it is necessary

that man should have a right judgment
concerning these truths, that he should
value his power of clinging to them and of
shrinking from their denial. Such judgment concerning divine things pertains to
the gift of wisdom, whilst such judgment
concerning created things pertains to the
gift of knowledge." *

Thus the highest operations of the intellect
become controlled and guided by the Holy
Spirit. These gifts have their root in charity.
Hence the greater one's charity is, so much the
keener will his insight be into supernatural
truths.

Now we can discern which is the better
method for a sane creative evolution, the method
of Bergson or the method of Newman and
Aquinas.

Look first at the creations of science. Have
they been accomplished by turning away from
the intellect and the outside world, and by forc-
ing intuition to bear on the flow of the " now "?
Columbus sees wood floating on the water and
discovers America. Stephenson sees the kettle
boiling and discovers the steam engine. Far-

---

* *Summa* 2a 2ae qu. 8, a. 6 corp.

man observes a bird flying and makes an aëroplane. Archimedes jumps into his bath, turns out the water, and discovers the law of specific gravity. Is the reason evident?

> Now we clap
> Our hands and cry " Eureka"

Every discovery of any value to mankind has been the result of an illation of the intellect based upon sensible experience. Sometimes the experience has been a short and simple one, but sometimes it is a long series of patient experiments. Marconi required long trial and continued inference to perfect wireless telegraphy. So also did Madame Curie for the discovery of radium. And so, too, Mendel for the discovery of his laws of inheritance.

But, it may be argued, these are instances of physical science merely. What about the real creations of art? Surely the greatest creations of painting have been inspired by a Mother and a Child. The most sublime works of sculpture have for their face value a woman or a man. So, too, in music, the very nature of which might seem to exclude images. Beethoven, in the depths of despair over his manuscript, hears a knock at the door: he waits and hears another, and these two knocks provide the theme for one of his superb symphonies. Bach takes the letters of his name, changes the H into G sharp, and writes one of his classical fugues. Palestrina adopts a simple melody from the plain chant, and upon that builds up the music of a Mass. All of which points to the universal axiom that genius is but an infinite capacity for taking pains.

But pains are just the things which the disciples of Bergson will not take. It is so much easier to say: " I believe in so and so, not because I can give any reason for it, but because I see it intuitively. If the rest of the world fails to see it, that is only because the rest of the world has not cultivated the higher sensitiveness."

Hence it is that in the world of art we have those *soi-disant* creators, the Futurists and Post-impressionists. Having thrust intellect aside, having destroyed all spatial values, and having projected their feeling into the flux of life, they have produced exactly that which one would expect them to produce, galleries of daubs and smudges.

Suppose a man imagines himself a superman,

beyond good and evil, and enunciates principles for which he has no reasonable justification—principles which he sees only by intuition—how are we to deal with him?

Many have done this; and chief amongst them is Friedrich Nietzsche. Nietzsche called himself the " creator of new values "; and his philosophy is the " transvaluation of all values." He retires to the upper regions of the Engadine, and shuts himself up within himself. Gradually his intuitions begin to enlarge. " Christ," he says, " is the first prophet of transvaluation, whereas I, Nietzsche, am the second prophet continuing the work of Christ. I have fulfilled Christ's work by destroying it." And so Nietzsche feels happy, free, light. He sees himself soaring to an infinite height above man; and believes his *creative thought* can do everything. " I am not a man; I am dynamite." In two years the earth will be in convulsive throes. But before this comes to pass his friends take pity upon him and place him under lock and key.

Perhaps the most obnoxious fruit of the Bergsonian philosophy is the work of M. Georges Sorel, the apostle of the general strike. From his quiet little home at Boulogne he sends forth effusions calculated to put whole nations into throes. His doctrines are only just beginning to make their way into England and America, though for some time they have influenced France, Italy, Spain, and Switzerland.

The general strike, or rather the threat of a general strike, is the weapon with which he is to renovate society. But this is not to be brought along by intellectual organisation, nor yet is it to be justified by a reasoned statement as to what will happen afterwards. Sorel pours contempt on such a scientific socialist as the English organiser, Mr Sidney Webb. His figures and statistics are indigestible; they require much time and trouble to assimilate.

Patience is not a characteristic virtue of the school of Bergson. Therefore Sorel seizes upon this intuitive method as an easy way of escaping the intellectual and moral difficulties which the concept of the general strike involves. Intuition, he says, is more than knowledge. If looking inward upon life, you see the general strike to be good or necessary, then intellectual analysis of the results becomes unnecessary. " Man has only genius in the measure that he does not reflect." The privilege of our personality is to impose itself on the future, and to cut into it without ceasing. Hence our intelligence cannot possibly anticipate what is going to happen.

Such ideas were readily taken up by the French syndicalists. Here was a ready-made apology for unchecked liberty to combine, and for a self-determined government heedless of all outward authority.

Indeed, Sorel goes further and distrusts socialist members of parliament and labour representation. He prefers the creative evolutionary methods of street demonstrations, strikes, boycotting, and sabotage. For to-day the Marxian doctrine of a materialistic conception of history is abandoned in favour of the creative evolution of Bergson.

When Sorel is asked what he will have if he rejects both intellectualism and materialism, he replies that he will depend on creative evolution. The people must revert to primitive states so as to get into instinctive and poetic moods. Bergson, he tells us, has done away with the rationalists, whilst any organised plan for the future is but the idol of politicians.

Is not the general strike an undivided whole?

G

How can it be possible to mark out the various parts of such a catastrophe as the transition from Capitalism to Socialism? Is it not a vital indivisible flowing continuum?

This last instance may serve as a lesson to those members of the orthodox camp, and there are many of them, who think that metaphysics has no connection with the practical life of the multitude. The filtering down is usually a process so intricate and so long that it is not easily observable. But here the passage is quick, requiring the minds of only two men to form a disastrous speculation to realise it.

Bergson upsets the concepts of " being " and " becoming "; then Sorel upsets railway-carriages and tram-cars. Bergson says: " Keep your intelligence for the humdrum things of every-day life, but use your intuition to evolve new creations." Sorel replies: " Yes, sire, I am doing it, and the Happy Land is coming."

Ah, but the essential condition of a happy and prosperous community is stability, whereas the essential characteristic of Bergsonian philosophy is instability or change. Therefore, not by this method can the Happy Kingdom come. A stable society can only be assured when wealth is divided amongst the majority of the citizens. But that is just what Syndicalism aims at frustrating.

Syndicalism, with true instinct, follows the philosophy which prescribes everlasting change, not only accidental change, but change of essence, change of the thing in itself. Sorel may well say that his Happy Land is coming. Perhaps it is. But it is coming in such a way that it will be *always* coming—it never can and never will arrive.

CHAPTER V

THE NEW IDEA OF FREEDOM

A DISLOCATION of the intellect of necessity involves a dislocation of the will. Hence it comes about that M. Bergson must formulate an entirely new doctrine concerning freedom. Hitherto the upholders and the opponents of free will have understood each other fairly well. There has been no doubt as to the point at issue. When two alternative courses of action are intelligently perceived, does the will possess a liberty of choice between them? The libertarians say Yea, whilst the determinists say Nay. But in this new philosophy the intellect is not considered to be the supreme judge and guide in conduct. The new conceptions of space and time and flow and intuition have changed all this. Both libertarians and determinists have been fighting over a problem which ought never to have existed. Freedom is not the choice between two alternatives proposed by the understanding. Freedom is a great creative act which is the result of the whole of a man's character. It is made but seldom and perhaps never in a man's lifetime. Once again M. Bergson has changed the standard coinage. He is said to have placed freedom in such a safety as it never was before. We contend that he has placed it in such a jeopardy as it never was before.

Before coming to real grips with M. Bergson it will be necessary to dispose of a preliminary misunderstanding. He seems not to have correctly grasped the scholastic doctrine. He poses a dilemma which comes to this: Either the will is moved by the strongest motive, in which case it is not free; or it is indifferent to motives, in which case the moral responsibility of the agent is destroyed. Now such is not a correct presentment of the state of the question. We propose then to give a brief description of the scholastic doctrine. The same will then serve as a norm by which to judge the various points of M. Bergson's doctrine.

We define the will as the faculty or appetite which strives after some good apprehended by the intellect. We define freedom as that active indifference of the will by which the agent, when all the conditions requisite for acting are present, is able either to put forth the volition or to abstain from doing so. Free-will therefore implies two things: first there must be some intellectual light present, and secondly that the volition is freely exerted by the agent and is not a necessary result of his nature or environment. Of course many of a man's acts during the day, indeed most of them, are the result of nature and of habit, which is the second nature. Most of a man's acts are the result of a predominant motive. The question before us, therefore, is not whether *all* a man's spontaneous actions are free or not, but only whether *some* of them are. The schoolmen then have a very important distinction to separate the two kinds of acts. When a human action is done, as we should say, deliberately and after reflection, it is called an *actus humanus*, but when it is done indeliberately, without reflex thought or by force of habit, then it is called an *actus hominis*. It is only the deliberate acts which we claim to be free.

Further we claim that in these deliberate acts the agent is to a certain extent influenced by motives. The function of his intelligence is to weigh evidence. And since there are two sides to every question there must be motives drawing him to either side. But the weightier motive is not enough to force his will one way. Probably he will follow the weightier motive, and an outsider who knew all the circumstances might foretell with the greatest probability which course he would take. But he could not foretell with certainty, because the freedom which is in the will defies exact calculation.

The first mistake of M. Bergson is in supposing that the question is one of either being determined by necessary causes or of being absolutely regardless of motives. There is a middle way. The will is influenced to a certain extent by evidence duly weighed by the intellect, but it is not absolutely determined by it. In the late crisis with the Church the French Government thought that it had laid down sufficient motives to incline Pope Pius X. towards its own desires. But it was out in its reckoning, for Pius X. being a man of free will, was able to do what he did, namely, just the thing which the French Government thought he would not do. Nevertheless, Pius X. was not without a motive for what he did. He had a motive, but was not of necessity determined by it.

Thus freedom is not the same thing as independence. To identify freedom with independence is to have the most false of all false notions of freedom. Real freedom is dependent at least upon some evidence but is not necessitated by it.

If an agent acts absolutely without any thought at all he is not acting freely, for having no motives he has nothing to choose from, whereas the very essence of freedom consists in choice.

The primary testimony of this freedom is an intuition of the strictest kind. If we look into ourselves and place ourselves between two alternatives, say to take up one book or another, or to take up a book or leave it alone, we can see immediately and without any discursive reasoning that we are able to choose. Moreover this consciousness of being able to choose freely is present before, during, and after the act. And this consciousness of freedom is so universal in mankind that it must be taken to be one of the essential features of human nature. If an individual here or there says that he has not got the consciousness he must be written down as an odd person and treated accordingly, or perhaps a philosopher may say that although he may have the first intuition of freedom yet by a chain of reasoning he can prove that he is not free. Then the answer is that the chain of reasoning depends ultimately on primary intuitions, and if the testimony of consciousness is not to be trusted when it shows forth freedom then neither can it be trusted when it shows forth the data from which the chain of reasoning begins.

Besides this direct consciousness of freedom there is also discursive proof of it. This lies in the responsibility which is universally attached to human acts. If a man's acts are all determined by heredity and environment then he himself cannot be held responsible. If a man jumps into the sea at the risk of his life to save a fellow-traveller, then, on the determinist principle, no praise is due to him, for he could not help it. So, too, if a man tells a lie and calumniates his neighbour, then, on the determinist principle, no blame is due to him, for he could not help it. But all sane mankind does praise acts of heroism and does blame acts of lying. Why? Because they believe the doers to be free agents, possessed of free choice, able to do these things or leave them undone according as they freely choose.

Thirdly the will may be shown to be necessarily free from the very limitations of our intellectual outlook. The will is an appetite which always tends toward that which is apprehended as good. Whatever good we think about, it is either difficult to obtain, or, if we obtain it, we are not sure of being able to keep it. Since then, everything which we can have in this life is both good in some respect and defective in some respect, the will must of necessity be free to pick and choose. Hence whichever way we look at freedom its existence depends upon intellectual light.

We are now in a position to approach M. Bergson's treatment of it. The determinists say that intellectual light destroys freedom, since it acts as a determining motive. M. Bergson says that they are right if we allow the intellect to be a motive at all. Therefore, if we would save freedom, we must seek for it somewhere else than in the choice between two alternatives each apprehended by the intellect. He proposes to find it in the very rare creative acts which are the expression of man's whole personality. And this is how he arrives at his conclusion.

The great bugbear which stands in the way of a solution of the problem is space. Psychic states pertain to real time, that all-important flowing " now," whereas space does not. Time flown may be represented by spatial pictures, but not so time flowing. But an act of freedom is a supreme psychic state. Therefore it cannot be measured, nor yet can it be compared with alternative courses proposed by the intellect.

" What I attempt to prove is," writes M. Bergson, " that all discussion between the determinists and their opponents implies a previous confusion of duration with exten-sity, of succession with simultaneity, of quality with quantity: this confusion once dispelled, we may perhaps witness the dis-appearance of the objections raised against free will, of the definitions given to it, and, in a certain sense of the problem of free will itself." *

About two-thirds of the volume treating par-ticularly of this subject is taken up in the attempt

* *Time and Free Will*, p. 19.

to show that psychic states are not subject to
the laws of mathematics and geometry, or in
other words, that if they can be said to be
greater or less, the difference is one of intensity
and not extensity.   If I am sorry my sorrow
is neither square nor round, and if I am glad
my gladness is neither seven nor eight.   If we
do attach magnitude to psychic states it is only
because the intellect, being normally at home
with solids, uses analogies of spatial magnitude
to represent that which has no space and no
measurement.   Psychic states simply endure in
an unceasing flow, and consequently any intellectual or pictorial representation of them is
entirely inadequate to the reality, and is but
an artificial device for the practical purposes of
life.

"We should, therefore, distinguish two
forms of multiplicity, two very different
ways of regarding duration, two aspects of
conscious life.   Below homogeneous duration, which is the extensive symbol of true
duration, a close psychological analysis
distinguishes a duration whose hetero-
geneous moments permeate one another;
below the self with well-defined states, a
self in which *succeeding each other* means

melting into one another and forming an organic whole. But we are generally content with the first, i.e. with the shadow of the self projected into homogeneous space. Consciousness goaded by an insatiable desire to separate, substitutes the symbol for the reality, or perceives the reality only through the symbol. As the self thus refracted, and thereby broken to pieces, is much better adapted to the requirements of social life in general and language in particular, consciousness prefers it, and gradually loses sight of the fundamental self." *

If, therefore, we are to observe where freedom lies, so it is contended, we must ever turn our eyes on these two aspects of self. The surface self which is intellectual and static must be subject to the laws of science, and consequently can not be free. Whereas the fundamental self being independent of space, independent of intellect must be free.

" In order to recover this fundamental self, as the unsophisticated consciousness would perceive it, a vigorous effort of

* *Time and Free Will*, p. 129.

analysis is necessary, which will isolate the fluid inner states from their image, first refracted, then solidified in homogeneous space. In other words, our perceptions, sensations, emotions and ideas occur under two aspects: the one clear and precise, but impersonal; the other confused, ever-changing, and inexpressible, because language cannot get hold of it, without arresting its mobility or fit it into its commonplace forms without making it into public property." *

Fixing our mental gaze on the fluid fundamental self we find there the kinetic action of the whole soul. There is the gathering up of the whole of the life-force.

" There is no need to associate a number of conscious states in order to rebuild the person, for the whole personality is in a single one of them, provided that we know how to choose it. And the outward manifestation of this inner state will be just what is called a free act, since the self alone will have been the author of it, and since it will express the whole of the self. Freedom, thus understood, is not *absolute*, as a

* *Time and Free Will*, p. 129.

radically libertarian philosophy would have it; it admits of degrees." *

Many people, it is admitted, do not allow their experiences to sink down into this fundamental self. If an education is not properly assimilated there grows up a parasitic self which continually encroaches upon the real self. People who allow this parasitic self to grow can never know what freedom is. They live merely by rule and routine and consequently are always determined.

Indeed, this would seem to be the case with the majority of mankind. Sad to say, most men are rational animals and mistake the spatial representation of time for the real fluid stuff, and hence " free acts are exceptional, even on the part of those who are most given to controlling and reasoning out what they do." †

Moreover, M. Bergson will go so far as to say that when an act is the result of this bubbling up of inner life, even though there be no reason whatever for it, nevertheless it may be a free act. Our quotation must be a long one but it

* *Time and Free Will*, pp. 165-166.
† *Ibid.*, p. 167.

is necessary if we are to appreciate the extent to which reason is prostituted in this philosophy.

"When our most trustworthy friends agree in advising us to take some important step, the sentiments which they utter with so much insistence lodge on the surface of our *ego* and there get solidified in the same way as the ideas of which we spoke just now. Little by little they will form a thick crust which will cover up our own sentiments; we shall believe that we are acting freely, and it is only by looking back to the past, later on, that we shall see how much we were mistaken. But then, at the very moment when the act is going to be performed, *something* may revolt against it. It is the deep-seated self rushing up to the surface It is the outer crust bursting, suddenly giving way to an irresistible thrust. Hence in the depths of the self, below this most reasonable pondering over most reasonable pieces of advice, something else was going on—a gradual heating and a sudden boiling over of feelings and ideas, not unperceived, but rather unnoticed. If we turn back to them and carefully scrutinise our memory we shall see that we had ourselves shaped these ideas, ourselves lived these feelings, but that, through some strange reluctance to exercise our will, we had thrust them back into the darkest depths of our soul whenever they came up to the surface. And this is why we seek in vain to explain our sudden change of mind, by the visible circumstances which preceded it. We wish to know the reason why we have made up our mind and we find that we have decided without any reason, and perhaps even against every reason. But in certain cases, that is the best of reasons. For the action which has been performed does not then express some superficial idea, almost external to ourselves, distinct and easy to account for; it agrees with the whole of our most intimate feelings, thoughts and aspirations, with that most particular conception of life which is the equivalent of all our past experience, in a word, with our personal idea of happiness and honour." *

Let us notice here that the force which is supposed to rise up and burst into freedom is indiscriminately composed of feelings and ideas.

* *Time and Free Will*, pp. 169-170.

H

Let us notice that we have two selves at variance
with each other. Let us note above all things
that the palm of freedom is given to blind inclination in preference to intellectual vision.
And all this is calmly assumed to be our highest
and noblest life, the quintessence of a life spent
in forming a happy and honourable character.

Then, of course, when intellect and space
have been excluded from the process, when the
free act has been placed in the fluid " now,"
when the faculty by which it is perceived is
declared to be only feeling, there must of necessity be some difficulty in defining what freedom
is. Indeed, M. Bergson says quite frankly that
it is indefinable. Since it springs from that deep
living flow of fundamental life, and not from
the superficial crust, it must be vague to the
understanding. If we attempted to define it we
should crystalise it and at once thereby concede
the whole case to the determinists. We must
therefore keep the concept nebulous. Clear-
ness is static whilst nebulosity is always shifting.

" Freedom must be sought in a certain
shade or quality of the action and not in
the relation of this act to what it is not

or to what it might have been. All the difficulty arises from the fact that both parties (determinists and libertarians) picture the deliberation under the forms of an oscillation in space, while it really consists in a dynamic progress in which the self and its motives, like real living beings, are in a constant state of becoming. The self, infallible when it affirms its immediate experiences, feels itself free and says so; but as soon as it tries to explain its freedom to itself it no longer perceives itself except by a kind of refraction through space. Hence a symbolism of a mechanical kind, equally incapable of proving, disproving or illustrating free will." *

The nearest approach to a definition is this, that freedom is the relation of the concrete self to the act which it performs. Just as there is some sort of indefinable resemblance between the work of an artist and the artist himself, so there is an indefinable resemblance between each concrete free act and the concrete agent who performs it.

" This relation is indefinable, just be-

* *Time and Free Will*, pp. 182-183.

cause we *are* free. For we can analyse a thing, but not a process; we can break up extensity but not duration. Or, if we persist in analysing it, we unconsciously transform the process into a thing and duration into extensity. By the very fact of breaking up concrete time we set out its moments in homogeneous space; in place of the doing we put the already done; and, as we have begun by, so to speak, stereotyping the activity of the self, we see spontaneity settle down into inertia and freedom into necessity. Thus, any positive definition of freedom will ensure the victory of determinism." *

It is a very strange admission on the part of a philosopher to say that he is actually unable to define his terms. To do this is to admit that he is cornered. We must, therefore, go over his steps again, see where he went wrong, and then perhaps we shall be able to define the corner in which we now observe him.

We begin with the evolutionary philosophy. From the initial thrust of creative evolution there has evolved man as we know him. Various

* *Time and Free Will*, pp. 219-220.

branches of life have bifurcated. Intellect is but a development of sensation which life itself has created for a purpose. Intellect and sensation are, therefore, always radically the same thing. Intellect is always extended. Hence M. Bergson is beset the whole time with the difficulty of trying to get away from extension.

Now if he had admitted at the beginning, as the schoolmen constantly teach, that there is an essential difference between intellect and sensation, he would not have impaled himself as he has done. We not only admit, but we claim and emphasise that the intellectual act is not quantitive. It transcends not only space *but time also*. Then if we are asked how the intellect manipulates the world of solids we answer that it is through the instrumentality of the phantasy. St. Thomas states this position so delicately and clearly that we cannot do better than repeat his words. He seems almost to have foreseen the speculations of M. Bergson.

" Distance in place," he says, " ordinarily affects sense, not intellect, except incidentally, where intellect has to gather its data from sense. For while there is a definite law of distance according to which sensible objects affect sense, terms of intellect, as they impress the intellect, are not in *place*, but are separate from bodily matter." *

Moreover, the intellect is able to transcend time as well.

"Terms of intellect are as independent of time as they are of place. Time follows upon local motion, and measures such things only as are in some manner placed in space. . . . Time is a condition of our intellectual activity since we receive knowledge from phantasms that regard a fixed time. Hence to its judgments, affirmative and negative, our intelligence always appends a fixed time, *except when it understands the essence of a thing*. It understands essence by abstracting terms of understanding from the conditions of sensible things; hence in that operation it understands irrespectively of time and other conditions of sensible things." †

Here St. Thomas puts the operations of the intellect beyond both space and time flown. Had

* *Contra Gentiles*, Lib. II., Cap XCVI.
† *Ibid*.

M. Bergson not been obsessed by his radical evolutionism he might have saved himself the trouble of writing the first two long chapters of his *Time and Free Will*. The free act is essentially independent of time and space. We grant him that, not because fluid time is not space, but because the acts of the intellect are simple, spiritual, unextended acts, and therefore, essentially beyond time and space. When the intellect has thus been rescued from the necessitous bonds of sensation it has been rescued from all determinist danger. When M. Bergson confuses intellect with sensation he first concedes with the right hand to the determinist that which he afterwards tries to take away with the left. There is no need for all these contortions. The intellect is essentially distinct from sense. We can *picture*, for instance, with the imagination an individual man, say President Wilson or ex-President Taft, and such an individual must have a definite size and shape. But we can also *think* of the universal concept "man" which has no definite size or shape, but which is applicable to every individual. If the intellect is only incidentally dependent on time and space in so far as it abstracts its universal concepts from particular phantasms which exist in time space, if essentially it is independent of time and space, then it can provide a spiritual motive for the will which can influence the will without necessitating it.

Even those of us who hold the traditional doctrine of free will need to be constantly on our guard against misunderstanding the use of the word "motive." We need constantly to remind ourselves that when we speak of the spirit we must needs do so in terms of the flesh. These terms, therefore, are analogical and are not quite adequate for their purpose. When we speak of motive-power applied by one spiritual faculty to another, it is not the same kind of motive-power as that which is applied by a sledge-hammer to a wedge. One is vital and spiritual whilst the other is mechanical and material. The latter is of its nature necessitous whilst the former of its nature is free.

M. Bergson has been obsessed by this confusion from the beginning to the end of his work. Thus he has been constrained to deny freedom to acts which hitherto have been considered free, and to attribute freedom to acts which may or may not be free.

" Hence it has been a mistake," he says, " to look for examples in the ordinary and even indifferent circumstances of life in order to prove that man is capable of choosing without a motive. It might easily be shown that these insignificant actions are bound up with some determining reason. It is at the great and solemn crisis, decisive of our reputation with others, and yet more with ourselves, that we choose in defiance of what is conventionally called a motive, and this absence of any tangible reason is the more striking the deeper our freedom goes." *

This continued attempt to obscure the intellectual life by an appeal to life as a whole, really an appeal to the whole life minus intellect, reaches the height of the picturesque, when M. Bergson tries to explain away our deliberation between two courses of action.

" In reality there are not two tendencies, or even two directions, but a self which lives and develops by means of its very hesitations, until the free action drops from it like an over-ripe fruit." †

* *Time and Free Will*, p. 170.
† *Ibid.*, p. 176.

Our first criticism of the foregoing doctrine will be an appeal to that very consciousness of living upon which M. Bergson depends so much. He appeals to that consciousness, and rightly so too, for evidence that some of our acts are free. But does not that very consciousness announce the possibility of choosing an alternative? And does not that very consciousness announce the same thing equally so before, during and after the act which is in fact chosen? If consciousness does not announce this, it announces nothing at all. If it is not valid against the determinists and in favour of their old opponents, then neither is it valid in favour of the freedom proposed by M. Bergson. The symbol of the fall of over-ripe fruit means that so many determining influences are acting upon it that it can no longer remain hanging on the tree, but must of necessity fall to the ground. Now that is just what our immediate consciousness tells us does not take place with regard to our free acts. That consciousness tells us that we could have kept the fruit hanging so long as we freely chose to do so.

Nor is M. Bergson any better off if we appeal to discursive reasoning. What sort of acts are they to which mankind attaches praise and blame? Which are the acts for which a person is held responsible, the deliberate ones or the impulsive ones?

First, for instance, take a prisoner who is charged with the capital offence. Let time and space enter very much into his deed. Let him be known to have traversed continents and to have taken weeks and months in which to mature his crime. Let him pass through all those acts which are indicative of intellectual deliberation. Let all this be proved against him and any jury will find him guilty without any recommendation to mercy. But on the other hand let him be known to have acted on the impulse of passion. Let him be known to be subject to brainstorms, those sudden outbursts of elemental passion, jealousy, anger and the like. Let it be proved that he acted without deliberation. Let it be shown that the beginning and the end of the process was in the fluid " now " (or " then "). The jury would undoubtedly hesitate to pronounce him guilty. It would declare rather that he was devoid of that intellectual light so necessary for freedom, and that consequently he was not fit to be numbered among free men, but must have accommodation provided for him in the safe institution at Manhattan.

Next let us take a case in which a great act is done at a crisis in a man's life, and which the world praises; let us say the conversion of Newman. Undoubtedly that act was the sum total of his past life, surface life as well as fundamental. Undoubtedly, influences were at work which he had forgotten. But then his mind was able to summarise his past thought. His will had framed volitional habits ever tending Godwards. And long years after the act he was able to go back on his past life and record the chief of the reasons which had urged him onward. He was able to write a whole book which was in the strictest sense of the word an *Apologia pro Vita Sua*. And who shall say that reason does not predominate in every line of it; yet it is not for the reasons which he gives that the world admires him. There are thousands upon thousands who admire his act whilst profoundly disagreeing with its reasons. It is because he acted in deference to conscience, because he could have remained where he was, but freely preferred to follow the " kindly light."

Then what shall we say of those whose past

life has been one of sin, and who suddenly become converted. Sin implies a direction away from God, whilst conversion implies the very opposite. We may take either St. Paul or St. Augustine or some of those non-Catholic varieties quoted by Professor William James. Are the free actions of these men to be compared with the fall of an over-ripe fruit; the whole trend and growth of the character of Paul had been towards the persecution of others. Then when the light suddenly came he was able to turn right about and begin an entirely new life. Self-development along the old lines would only have taken him further and further away from the free life which was afterwards to be such a joy to him.

St. Augustine has left us an account of passions tending to determine him one way and of freely fighting against them. But he requires time and space and something else. An outside free Power must raise and accentuate his own freedom.

> " I will plant my feet firmly on the ground where my parents placed me, until the evident truth be discovered. . . . Let me plan out my time; let me set apart fixed

hours for the salvation of my soul. . . . While I talked like this and the wind kept shifting and driving my heart now hither now thither, time was slipping away; I delayed my conversion to the Lord; I adjourned from day to day the life in Thee, but daily death in myself I could not adjourn. I loved the blessed life, but feared to seek it in its own abode; and I fled from it, while I sought it. For I thought I should be miserable without the embraces of a woman. I never gave a thought to the medicine which Thy mercy has provided for the healing of that infirmity, because I had never tasted it, and fancied that continence depended on our own strength. Such strength I was conscious that I did not possess, and, in my folly, I knew not how it is written: ' None can be continent unless Thou give it.' Certainly Thou wouldst have given it, if with unuttered groanings I had besieged Thine ears, and with firm faith had cast my care upon Thee." *

Then outside Catholicism there is the case which Newman describes as " the almost miraculous conversion and subsequent life of Colonel

* *Confessions*, Bk. VI. chap. xi.

Gardiner." * Professor James speaks of it as "the classic case of Colonel Gardiner," the man who was cured of sexual temptation in a single hour. To Mr Spears the Colonel said : " I was effectually cured of all inclination to that sin I was so strongly addicted to that I thought nothing but shooting me through the head could have cured me of it; and all desire and inclination to it was removed, as entirely as if I had been a sucking child; nor did the temptation return to this day." † Mr Webster's words on the same subject are these ; " One thing I have heard the Colonel frequently say, that he was much addicted to impurity before his acquaintance with religion ; but that so soon as he was enlightened from above, he felt the power of the Holy Ghost changing his nature so wonderfully that his sanctification in this respect seemed more remarkable than in any other." ‡

In presenting these examples let us beware of a possible Bergsonian retort that these lives were one continous flow, and that conversion was but a curve in the direction. The question

---

* *Difficulties of Anglicans*, Vol. I. p. 91.
† *Varieties of Religious Experience*, p. 269.
‡ *Ibid.*, p. 269.

we are dealing with at present is not the flow but the freedom. M. Bergson places freedom in the gathering up and bursting of a particular kind of life. But if this were true then a sinful course of life ought to fructify in sin, and the free act should be a sinful act falling from the sinner like over-ripe fruit. But in the case just quoted it is precisely the contrary that happens. The act of conversion, instead of being the ripe fruit of past conduct, is the beginning of a new life. The continuum is broken. The new life is discontinuous from the old, being of an entirely different order. Nay, it is the very discontinuity that is counted as meritorious. The freedom and responsibility were present, for the world does not praise where there is no responsibility. Nor does the presence of grace, admitted in all three cases, lessen the responsibility or deprive the agents of merit.

It remains for us now to do for M. Bergson that which he has declined to do for himself, namely to define his so-called freedom. The only vestige of freedom which he has retained is the name. The thing itself he has utterly sponged out from his method. The thing which he calls freedom is the act which is the result of all the powers of the soul. This might possibly be a free act if all the powers of the soul were reviewed by the intelligence and under intellectual light found expression through the will. But then, on the other hand, M. Bergson excludes the intellectual light. On one page he asks for the activity of the whole soul, whilst on the next page it is the whole soul minus intelligence which he requires. The difference between the Bergsonian crisis and the old determinist crisis is like that between the crisis of the modern motor-car and the old stage-coach. If the old stage-coach went smash, why there you were, but if the modern motor-car goes smash, why where are you? The brute beasts act in response to their whole souls. When the tiger is enraged, the whole gamut of his feelings is actuated and his resolves fall from his individuality like over-ripe fruit. And if we exclude the deliberations of the intellect from resolutions of man, the " whole soul " which is left is precisely similar to that of the tiger. So this is the definition which we must impose on Bergsonian freedom—sheer animal impulse. Indeed, in his later work, he seems to accept this conclusion.

I

" We have already said that animals and
vegetables must have separated soon from
their common stock, the vegetable falling
asleep in immobility, the animal, on the
contrary, becoming more and more awake
and marching to the conquest of a nervous
system. Probably the effort of the animal
kingdom resulted in creating organisms
still very simple, but endowed with a certain
freedom of action, and above all with a
shape so undecided that it could lend itself
to any future determination. These animals
may have resembled some of our
worms. . . . " *

In this case there is no difference whatever
between freedom and necessity. Determinism
triumphs but in the name of freedom.

It is not difficult to see the effect of this
philosophy on other manifestations of the time-
spirit of which it is itself the outcome. If this
new concept of freedom be true then the doctrine
of man's self-perfectibility is absolute and final,
mere sensation is the norm of morality, and man
is locked up for ever in pure subjectivism. The
new thing does not shew itself under these ugly
names but clothes itself with such terms as " self-

* *Creative Evolution*, p. 136.

realisation," "enchantment of life," "living out one's own nature."

Looked at more closely the new thing is found to be composed chiefly of the three appetites: for gold, sex, and independence respectively. When the *élan vital* appears as the lust for gold it sets up the banner of freedom of contract. If it can only play upon, or rather prey upon the poor man's need of bread it ignores all sense of the real thing freedom. Lust determines the signature of the contract on the one part and hunger determines the signature of the contract on the other.

When the vital impulse thrusts itself onward under the form of sexual appetite it does so in the name of love. It even counts as immoral any attempt to keep this love within any constraining limits of law. " He who feels strongly enough " writes Ellen Key, " does not ask himself whether he has a right to that feeling—he is so enlarged by his love that he feels the life of humanity is enlarged by him." The pity is that those who adopt such teaching find out their mistake when it is too late. The surrender to erotic excitement is the passing from personal liberty into abject slavery, and there is no need to describe further the lamentable results of it.

When the creative evolution expands as the lust for independence there is no sphere of life that it may not vitiate. Everywhere law is needed to protect personal freedom from the intrusion of undue determining forces. But the lust for independence is impatient of all law. Independence is therefore the great enemy of freedom. If freedom is to reign, the lust for independence must be kept within bounds of reason. And this must be done immediately and constantly, for the more the passion is allowed independence the more it grows in intensity, and the less reason and will are exercised in controlling it so much the weaker do these faculties become. The appetites for gold, sex, and independence are not bad things in themselves. They are the spontaneous motor-forces which are designed to carry on the existence of the race. But, lest they should be dissipated in aimless diffusion, laws are needed to economise them.

We cordially agree, therefore, with M. Bergson that the whole problem of free will harks back to the question: Is time space? We

agree with him that time is not space. But we
profoundly disagree with him in divorcing time
from space as he does. They are indissolubly
wedded together. And I speak here not merely
of space and time flown, but of space and time
flowing. Flowing time has no meaning unless
there be moving bodies with which to measure
it. But space is an essential quality of moving
bodies. Space, therefore, is wanted to give
definition to what would be a vague and
nebulous idea of flowing time. Nay, the problem rather harks further back to the most
elementary question of all: Is " being " identical
with " becoming " ? It is not. But " being " is
needed for " becoming." Before we can treat
of " becoming " as a reality at all we must first
satisfy ourselves that it *is*. Similarly we must
run this metaphysical principle through the
whole course of our reasoning. As " being " is
wanted for " becoming," so is the static wanted
for the kinetic, so is space wanted for time, so
is reason wanted for will, so is authority wanted
for autonomy, and so is law wanted for freedom.
Yes, even in the simplest acts of free will some
laws must be observed. Even if it be such a
simple choice as to whether I shall stand up

or sit down, law must be taken into account. It will not do for me to yield to any inclination whatsoever and tumble about anywhere. I must reckon with the law of gravity for instance and the equilibrium of forces. Otherwise I might sit down to my unexpected discomfiture.

CHAPTER VI

FINALISM

ONE of the characteristics of the time-spirit is that its consciousness is centred on means without reference to their end. We have already seen how the masters in Eugenics invite us to adopt any ideal we like, provided only we use Eugenic methods to attain it. Almost the whole of our County Council education is carried out on the same principle. Ask the members of our education committees what they aim at in deciding the curriculum of their schools and they will be puzzled for an answer. After some reflection they may tell you that their aim is to produce an English gentleman. But ask them what constitutes an English gentleman, and they will be puzzled again. So too is it with the rush of commerce. Doubtless money-making is the proximate end of it all, though even here some men are so absorbed in the process itself as to ignore even the proximate end. They do not balance their accounts and consequently wake up some fine morning to find themselves bankrupt. Nay, this would seem to be a tendency of all human nature, for it is evident even in religion, where the end is professedly fixed in another world. The parish priest, devoted to his people, tends to make his parish work the end of all things. A society for the propagation of catholic truth tends to regard its own interests as paramount. Even daily Communion may be exalted into an end in itself. Hence from time to time we have to check ourselves, to remind ourselves that these things are but means to an end, and to remember that the final end of man is to praise God and to serve Him throughout eternity.

Fundamentally the tendency is not bad. He who really wishes for the end wishes also for the means, so that he who is careless about the means is really not serious about attaining the end. The tendency to concentrate force on the means provides the driving-power which keeps the process going. It consists first of deliberate intention but afterwards becomes a kind of instinct and habit. The function of such habit

and instinct is to set free our deliberate intention so that it may look towards the final end
and seek out still more efficient means of attaining it. This requires constantly renewed effort.
To neglect this effort is to fall into the abuse of
making means an end in themselves.

M. Bergson's doctrine of finalism panders to
this abuse. We do not say it was designed for
this purpose. But we do say that it is the
natural outcome of his anti-intellectualism,
which is but the formulation of the time-spirit's
disinclination to reflect. Let us see what the
doctrine is.

First, the evolution progress such as we
have previously described is taken for granted.
Then an inquiry is instituted as to how this
transformation may be interpreted. Hitherto
we have had two chief interpretations set before
us, mechanism and finalism. The one is a
complexus of blind forces working out mechanically and by chance. The other is the realisation of an intelligent plan fixed beforehand.
Both, however, have failed to interpret the
history of evolution because both have been
weighted with the same fallacy. Neither has
taken into account the fact that the process is a

flux incapable of intellectual representation. There is just a grain of truth in the finalist explanation. M. Bergson leans slightly towards this.

> " We try on the evolutionary progress," he says, " two ready-made garments that our understanding puts at our disposal, mechanism and finality; we show that they do not fit, neither the one nor the other, but that one of them might be re-cut and re-sewn, and in this new form fit less badly than the other." *

The theory of creative evolution would, of course, exclude every form of mechanism. M. Bergson's criticism, indeed, of the various forms of mechanism is deadly in the extreme.

> " The mechanistic philosophy is to be taken or left: it must be left if the least grain of dust, by straying from the path foreseen by mechanics, should show the slightest trace of spontaneity." †

But spontaneity is observable everywhere.

* *Creative Evolution*, pp. xiv-xv.
† *Ibid.*, p. 42.

The comparison of the human eye with that of the Pecten is a most marvellous and conclusive proof that these organs have not been formed by the mechanical exigencies of environment. The Pecten is a mollusc commonly known as the scollop. Its eye is just as perfectly developed as that of any of the vertebrates. How is it that with such entirely different environments such similar results should be obtained? Consider the extremely complex structure of the eye together with its extremely simple function. It is composed of several parts such as the sclerotic, the retina, the crystalline lens, etc. Each one of these parts is divided into an almost infinite number of distinct parts. The retina, for instance, contains three layers of nervous elements—multipolar cells, bipolar cells, and visual cells—each of which is in itself a very complicated organism. Yet all these complexities are co-ordinated for the one simple act of vision. The slightest mistake in the vast system of co-ordination would have made sight impossible. And this co-ordination has been as perfectly accomplished in the mollusc as in man. Mechanism might account for the construction of one of these infinitesimal parts, but it throws no light whatever on their wondrous co-ordination.

The rejection of mechanism, however, involves the acceptation of some sort of finalism. M. Bergson even goes so far as to admit the necessity of some kind of direction over and above that of individual effort in order to account for variation.

" To sum up," he says, " if the accidental variations that bring about evolution are insensible variations, some good genius must be appealed to—the genius of the future species—in order to preserve and accumulate these variations, for selection will not look after this. If, on the other hand, the accidental variations are sudden, then, for the previous function to go on or for a new function to take its place, all the changes that have happened together must be complementary. So we have to fall back on the good genius again, this time to obtain the *convergence of simultaneous* changes, as before to be assured of the *continuity of direction* of *successive* variations." *

Naturally we must ask who this good genius

* *Creative Evolution*, p. 72.

may be.   Then we are referred to our old friend
the vital effort.   When hereditary changes take
place in definite directions, when each accumu-
lation is the building up of a more and more
complex machine, there must be an effort somewhere.   Nor can this effort be confined to
individual effort.   It must be something deeper,
and far more independent of circumstances.   It
must be " an effort common to most representa-
tives of the same species, inherent in the germs
they bear rather than in their substance alone,
an effort thereby assured of being passed on to
their descendants.   So we come back, by a
somewhat roundabout way, to the idea we
started from—that of an *original impetus* of life,
passing from one generation of germs to the
following generation of germs through the
developed organisms which bridge the interval
between the generations."*

Thus this vital impulse gnaws into the future,
sometimes creating more and more complex
forms and rising to higher and higher destinies,
but sometimes indeed resting not merely for
years or even centuries but for whole geological
periods.

* *Creative Evolution*, p. 92.

"Certain Foraminifera have not varied since the Silurian epoch. Unmoved witnesses of the innumerable revolutions that have upheaved our planet, the Lingulae are to-day what they were at the remotest times of the paleozoic era." *

M. Bergson may call his vital impulse a good genius or anything else he likes. If it is able to create the various species ranging from the amoeba up to man, and if it is able to abstain from creating and to rest in the Lingulae for aeons of time, then it must know something about the making of plans. So far he has delivered us from mechanism but not from finalism.

Why, then, does he object to finalism? He is obsessed by his singular views on the nature and function of time. If there is such a thing as a plan according to which the universe moves, then there is no use for time. There are no new forms for it to create, for practically everything has been already created. If the plan is given to begin with, then teleology is but mechanism inverted. The only difference between the two is that finalism puts our supposed

* *Creative Evolution*, p. 107.

guiding light in front of us whilst mechanism
puts it behind us. One acts as an attraction
whilst the other acts as an impulsion. Succession and movement and life remain but mere
appearances. If forms are foreseen in a general
plan, then they are not really created by the
flux of time. True, there is a certain amount
of contingency in finalism which does not obtain
in radical mechanism, and for that reason final
ism is to be preferred to its opponent. If, however, we must accept some sort of finalism, and
yet not that which supposes a general plan conceived and willed beforehand, what sort of
finalism does M. Bergson propose?

His thesis may be stated as follows: The
vital impulse which carries on the evolutionary
process starts off without any preliminary plan.
In the effort of ascending life to overcome
descending matter certain problems present
themselves. The vital impulse freely resolves
each problem in turn by creating absolutely new
forms, forms so absolutely new that they could
not have been foreseen even by an infinite
intellect.

This thesis has certain vague characteristics.
That the vagueness is not ours will perhaps be

evident if we call attention to the fact that we are not told whether the problems present themselves in intelligible terms or in unintelligible mist. Certainly there is supposed to be a clash between life and matter. That might conceivably produce smoke. But perhaps M. Bergson's own statement of his thesis may be clearer than ours.

"But," he says, "if the evolution of life is something other than a series of adaptations to accidental circumstances, so also it is not the realisation of a plan. A plan is given in advance. It is represented or at least representable, before its realisation. The complete execution of it may be put off to a distant future, or even indefinitely; but the idea is none the less formulable at the present time in terms actually given.

"If, on the contrary, evolution is a creation unceasingly renewed, it creates as it goes on, not only the forms of life, but the ideas which will enable the intellect to understand it, the terms which will serve to express it. That is to say that its future overflows its present and cannot be sketched out therein in an idea. There is the first error of finalism." *

* *Creative Evolution*, p. 108.

The first reason given for the rejection of a preliminary general plan is that it is too anthropomorphic, and is too much at variance with the observed operations of nature. The labour of nature, it is said, is made too much like that of a workman who chooses first a piece from here and then a piece from there, and eventually puts all into one construction according to an idea or a plan or a model which he has before his mind from the beginning. But if we look at embryonic life we find that it works quite another way. *"Life does not proceed by the association and addition of elements, but by dissociation and division."* *

The process here referred to is, of course, the well-known method of cell division. First a mother cell is formed. This splits up into two cells. Then these divide into two others, and so on until a complete organ is formed. But when a carpenter wishes to make a chair he does not begin by splitting himself up, and so on. Such is the force of M. Bergson's argument.

In reply we point out first that the organism of a cell is an organism. It has been organised. It contains definite potentialities. These poten-

* *Creative Evolution*, p. 94. Italics are M. Bergson's.

K

tialities must first have been put into it before they can actualise out. Then when they begin to actualise out they do so on a plan which can be foreseen with infallible certitude. I know, for instance, that the embryonic cell of a horse will not divide out into a cow. Nor will bantam eggs plan out into ducklings. All this is conclusive proof of a pre-arranged and foreseeable plan.

Moreover, even in the matter of choice of material, M. Bergson's comparison of nature with a workman tells in favour of finalism in its complete sense. Before life can proceed by dissociation and division, it must first proceed by association and addition of elements. Before the mother cell can make even one single division it must assimilate its distinctive food and nutrition. If it is an animal cell, it must assimilate phosphorous for the formation of nerve tissue. If it is a plant cell it must assimilate carbon for the formation of wood tissue.

Such power of assimilation implies a pre-arranged plan. The results too are foreseeable. I know with infallible certitude that if men breathe nothing but carbonic acid gas, and that if plants breathe nothing but pure oxygen, all will surely die. The plan conceived in advance must be followed if life is to have a fruitful issue.

Again, argues M. Bergson, if the course of nature is nothing more than a plan in course of realisation, then the future is closed. But in the evolution of life the portals must remain wide open, else there will be no opportunity for the creation of new forms. The unity of life is found solely in the impetus that pushes it along the road of time. The harmony is behind, not in front. There are too many failures in nature to admit of a preconceived plan. There are minor paths in the evolutionary push, deviations, arrests, and setbacks. The meaning of these can only be found in the virtue of the initial movement.

> "This movement constitutes the unity of the organised world—a prolific unity, of an infinite richness, superior to any that the intellect could dream of, for the intellect is only one of its aspects or products." *

Let us freely admit that the future is closed whilst the plan is being realised. But what about the future before the plan began its

* *Creative Evolution*, p. 110.

realisation? And what about the future after the plan is realised? Surely the portals have been and will be wide open. It is only the immediate future that is closed so that the world may be carried on intelligently.

When a carpenter begins to make a chair he usually intends to finish it. If he decided to leave the future open so that he might be always creating new forms he would never get any further. He must do one thing at once. He must not start first a chair, then a table, then a step-ladder, then a picture-frame, and so on, never realising a definite plan, and all under fear of closing the future. If he does this, neither chairs, tables, step-ladders, nor picture-frames will evolve at all.

Nor could nature thus keep the future open. Suppose the future were not closed to a bantam egg. And suppose the embryo began first by evolving towards a bantam, then changed its future to a duckling, then after two weeks incubation thought of becoming a kitten, and finally decided to be a puppy, what a funny thing it would look when it was born.

No. Both nature and art require a definite plan—foreseeable and foreseen. And what is true of the transformation of parts of the universe is true also of the whole. Certainly a human intellect can not see the correlation of all the parts, but the intellect of the Creator can. The God who transcends nature lives in eternity. With Him there is one eternal present. What with us is past, present, and future is as one only present to Him. Thus it is not strictly correct to speak of God *foreseeing* things. By one single intuition He sees directly that which is to us past, present, and future. He sees at once both the proximate end and the final end of every creature.

Nay, there can be no system of evolution at all intelligible which does not involve finalism right from the beginning to the end. When the initial impulse, postulated by M. Bergson, first started off, either it did so in a definite direction or it did not. If it had a definite direction it had a goal. If it had no direction, it never started. Whichever way you take it, you must either go somewhere or stay where you are. To start off for *nowhere*, as Bergsonian philosophy teaches, is a contradiction in terms.

Further, a theory of proximate ends implies a theory of an ultimate end. Let us grant for a moment that the semi-finalism proposed by M. Bergson is coherent. Let us suppose that the vital impulse can create both ideas and forms for its immediate needs without reference to any exemplar. Even so, there is required an ultimate and complete finalism in order to give meaning to the proximate semi-finalism which we have supposed.

The doctrine of semi-finalism declares that the vital impulse solves particular problems according to the measure in which they present themselves. But then, if they are to be rightly solved, they must be solved in view of the final problem of which they are a part or to which they are related. If, for instance, the complex structure of the eye finds its meaning in the simple act of vision, it but raises the problem as to what is the purpose of vision. If vision is for the purpose of enabling man to seek his food, then that gives rise to the problem as to what is the purpose of feeding. Thus we can go on pushing one problem against another. We eat in order that we may live. At length comes the final problem: why does man exist at all? There must be some reason for it. Seeing, walking, eating, and digesting must have

an ultimate purpose. And if the vital impulse
does not act according to this ultimate purpose,
how can it ordain intermediate functions to
attain it? If it has not got a plan of the whole
to guide it from start to finish how can it create
parts which will afterwards fit each other and
make up an intelligible whole?

Almost in spite of himself M. Bergson
stumbles into this incoherence again and again.
He thrusts out the general plan with his right
hand, but only to drag it in with his left. Nor
does his right hand know what his left hand does.

Let us take, for instance, the march of the
eye towards perfect vision. In the Infusorian
the eye is a mere pigment-spot which is im-
pressionable to light. The action is almost
purely chemical. Now this pigment-spot is
supposed to progress in perfection until it is as
perfect as the human eye. Its evolution takes
place either by slight or by sudden variations.
If by slight variations, what is their function?
Surely they are means to an end, stepping-
stones to more perfect vision. But if that end
is unknown and unforeseeable how can the
variations vary in the right direction? If there
is no goal at which to aim, why does not the

pigment-spot develop into an ear or a nose rather than into an eye?

Nor is the difficulty any less if the variations are sudden. Why should a pigment-spot make leaps along a particular line of evolution and eventually turn out to be an eye in its last sudden metamorphosis? There is no answer to this except that there was a definite aim in the evolution. The animal wanted to see better, and the more complex eye was the more apt instrument for this purpose.

But there is another serious consideration to be taken into account in the development of the eye. This organ does not float about in mid-air. It is an organism of an organism. It is fixed in the socket of an animal, and it is in vital connection with the brain, the heart, the stomach and the nerves. This connection has to be duly taken into account all through its evolution. A decaying tooth, for instance, may be the cause of an abscess growing on the eye. There is a co-ordination between the various members of the body which has to be kept in view during the whole time of development, else vision will be impossible. If one member suffer all the members suffer with it.

There must, therefore, be a general plan of the whole animal before the eye can be properly adjusted to the other organs which serve it, and which in turn it serves.

But further, the animal itself has to observe a plan of the world outside itself. If a man with a shooting-party is so careless or so disobedient as to go beyond the bounds set by the head keeper he runs the risk of getting a pellet in his eye. The eye is related not only to the various organs of the animal to which it belongs, but also to the whole universe. A speck of meteoric dust may easily put it out of action. Each individual problem which presents itself directly to the vital impulse leads sooner or later to the ultimate problem. A semi-finalism is meaningless without a complete finalism.

There is one more illustration used by M. Bergson which seems to us to gather up the whole of his contentions, and also, we may add, the whole of his fallacies. Let us quote it at length:

> "With greater precision" he says "we may compare the process by which nature constructs the eye to the simple act by which we raise the hand. But we supposed

at first that the hand met with no resistance.
Let us now imagine that, instead of moving
in air, the hand has to pass through iron
filings which are compressed, and offer
resistance to it in proportion as it goes
forward. At a certain moment the hand
will have exhausted its effort, and at this
very moment, the filings will be massed and
co-ordinated in a certain definite form, to
wit, that of the hand that is stopped and a
part of the arm. Now, suppose that the
hand and the arm are invisible. Lookers-
on will seek the arrangement in the filings
themselves and in the forces within the
mass. Some will account for the position
of each filing by the action exerted upon it
by the neighbouring filings: these are the
mechanists. Others will prefer to think
that a plan of the whole has presided over
the detail of these elementary actions: they
are the finalists. But the truth is that there
has been merely one indivisible act, that of
the hand passing through the filings; the
inexhaustible detail of the movement of the
grains, as well as the order of their final
arrangement, expresses negatively, in a
way, this undivided movement, being the
unitary form of a resistance and not a synthesis of positive elementary actions. For

this reason, if the arrangement of the grains is termed an ' effect ' and the movement of the hand a ' cause,' it may indeed be said that the whole of the effect is explained by the whole of the cause, but to parts of the cause parts of the effect will in no wise correspond. In other words, neither mechanism nor finalism will here be in place." *

A crab was once defined by an eminent scientific society as a red fish that walks backwards. The definition was correct except that a crab is not red, not a fish, and does not walk backwards. There are similar discrepancies in the statement of M. Bergson just quoted.

When the hand passes through the filings there has not been merely one act, nor has that act been indivisible. M. Bergson began by saying that the filings should be pressed and that they should offer resistance. There, at least, are two distinct acts, over and above that of the hand, both directed according to a plan. Moreover, the filings, when they were first filed, were filed according to a plan. They obeyed laws, some filing off one shape, others another.

* *Creative Evolution*, pp. 99-100.

When, therefore, the hand pushes through them, it pushes its way into a plan. It does so intelligently. Its action is divisible, for the owner of the hand can stop pushing at any moment he chooses. He chooses to go on until he is exhausted. Besides, there is the force of gravity acting on each of the filings and on the hand. All bodies attract and are attracted by all other bodies.

Since then there are so many forces acting, all conducing to one state of equilibrium, the final arrangement of the filings must express all these forces. It cannot be said to express merely the push of the hand. And, since there is no effect without a cause, each part of the total effect will correspond to each part of the total cause. Thus the free agent knows that if he thrusts his hand into the filings a second time to the same extent as he did previously, the same shape of filings will result. The form is foreseeable.

English admirers of M. Bergson, men who have been attracted by his theories of change and intuition, have been invariably brought to a check by his doctrine of finalism.

Our philosopher-statesman, Mr A. J. Balfour, boggles at it. Sir Oliver Lodge tries to explain it away, but in doing so he gives away the whole case to finalism :

> " Yet there is clearly an aim in all this, and life is always subject to its own laws. There is a controlling entity in a seed whereby the same product results, no matter amid what surroundings. If an acorn can grow at all, an oak results." *

But in the process of creative evolution this principle is just what is denied by M. Bergson. The controlling entity does not exist beforehand, but is created to meet a particular problem at a particular crisis. The concept of flowing time excludes the concept of controlling laws. These belong to the artificial sphere of intellect, not to the vital sphere of intuitive vision. Sir Oliver may be true to the facts of his own science, but he is not true to the theories of M. Bergson.

Mr Balfour would seem to have read the new philosopher with more care. Thus does he sum up and dispose of the new theory of finalism :

> " But why should he banish teleology?

* _Hibbert Journal_, Jan. 1912, p. 306.

In his philosophy superconsciousness is so indeterminate that it is not permitted to hamper itself with any purpose more definite than that of self-augmentation. It is ignorant not only of its course, but of its goal; and for the sufficient reason that, in M. Bergson's view, these things are not only unknown but unknowable. But is there not a certain incongruity between the substance of such a philosophy and the sentiments associated with it by its author? Creation, freedom, will—these doubtless are great things; but we cannot lastingly admire them unless we know their drift. We cannot, I submit, rest satisfied with what differs so little from the haphazard; joy is no fitting consequent of efforts which are so nearly aimless. If values are to be taken into account, it is surely better to invoke God with a purpose, than supra-consciousness with none." *

It is most remarkable that when St. Thomas treats of this question of finalism he begins with the identical difficulty proposed by M. Bergson.

" It would seem " he says in proposing

* *Hibbert Journal*, Oct. 1911, p. 23.

the objection, "that God is not the final cause of all things, for to act on account of an end would seem to imply that the agent was in need of something. But God is in need of nothing, therefore He does not act for the sake of an end." *

In answer to this, St. Thomas first quotes the inspired word that "the Lord hath made all things for Himself." †

This he takes on faith, and then sets his faith to seek to understand.

"Every agent" he says "acts for the sake of an end. Otherwise from any given action neither this particular thing nor that would happen, except by chance. But there are some agents which both act and are acted upon. These are imperfect agents, and whenever they act they must intend to acquire some new perfection. But the first agent, who acts only and is not acted upon, does not act for the sake of attaining to some end, but intends only to communicate His own perfection, which

* *Summa*, pars. 1a, qu. xliv., a. iv. diff. I.
† *Prov.* xvi. 4.

is His own goodness. Thus, therefore, the divine goodness is the end of all things. Wherefore to act on account of a need is but the action of an imperfect agent, which is made to act and to be acted upon. But this is not so with God's action. So it is that He alone is supremely generous, for He does not act for His own benefit, but merely on account of His goodness."

It is in the divine goodness then that we must seek for the root of the divine finalism. He who is the beginning of creatures is also their end. "I am the Alpha and Omega." God being perfectly happy in Himself could not desire an additional perfection. He could only desire to communicate His goodness to others. Such communication would be an outward imitation of His own intrinsic perfections. God Himself, therefore, is the plan or ideal upon which the universe was formed.

Whenever anything is produced, there is evident need of an exemplar so that the effect may have some definite form. Hence all created things may be traced to their first principle, the Divine Wisdom which thought out the order of the universe. In the Divine

Wisdom are to be sought the reasons of all things. The ideas which are their exemplar are found in the divine mind. Of course these ideas are only separate from each other in so far as they are realised or realisable in the created world. In the divine mind they are identical with each other and identical with the divine goodness and identical with divine essence. But as there can only be one infinite, the outward representation of the divine ideal must be finite and inadequate. Hence each separate creature is a finite likeness of the infinite divine essence.

Let us ask ourselves now what we commonly understand by the word " prudence." A prudent man is one who has a good memory of past events, who is able to grasp a large present situation, and from his knowledge of past and present is able to make plans against future contingencies. The man who knows the first principles of things who is able to co-ordinate his principles into general knowledge, and who can apply his general knowledge for the attainment of some desirable end is said to be eminently wise.

But God can do all these things with one

thought and one volition. He therefore is wise and prudent supereminently. He therefore can and does exercise a providence over His created world, adapting right means to right ends, co-ordinating and subordinating all proximate and intermediate ends to the one final end. What we understand by " prudence " or " wisdom " or " providence " in man is realised in God infinitely. Hence we have the classic definition of divine providence—*ipsa divina ratio in summo omnium principe constituta quae cuncta disponit*—the all-regulating and stable plan of God, the supreme ruler of the universe.

Moreover, the God who is infinitely perfect is unchangeable. Change would imply the acquisition of a new perfection. Since, therefore, God is unchangeable, He must have settled from all eternity the final goal to which all His creatures should be directed.

Again, since His wisdom existed from eternity He must from eternity have fixed the various ways by which these creatures should come to their ultimate end. He not only has set Himself a plan, but He also has applied His intelligence and will to the working out of the plan in such a way that nothing shall happen to prevent His desire from being realised.

At this point we must distinguish carefully between that which God approves, and that which, for good reasons, He merely tolerates. He approves of good acts, whilst He only tolerates or permits bad acts. When we speak of God tolerating or permitting sin, we do not mean that He gives permission to sin, but only that He does not hinder the creature from exercising his free will in sinning. God could hinder it, but does not, and so we speak of Him as tolerating it. With this distinction before our minds, we are able to lay down the principle that whatever happens in the world, happens according to the will of God, positively or permissively.

Thus then, does the eternal Father preside over His own creation. There is neither a sun nor a grain of dust, not the cry of a bird nor the fall of a snow-flake, not a human thought nor a human desire which escapes His all-wise and all-loving control. Every created movement is subordinated to one final plan, known and willed eternally by God.

This external representation of divine per-

fections is called the external glory of God. His
internal glory can be known to none but Himself.
In so far as creatures, by their existence and
activity, are apt to manifest some divine perfection, they are said to render a material glory to
God. " The heavens show forth the glory of
God, and the firmament declareth the work of
His hands." And when intelligent beings,
seeing the reflections of the divine perfections in
creation, acknowledge them in thought, word
and deed, then they are said to render formal
glory to God. Thus all parts of creation,
rational and irrational, have this for their final
end to make one harmonious hymn of praise to
their Creator.

Hence the finalism which we adopt is the very
antithesis of mechanism, direct or inverted.
The very nature of the ideal and of the means
of realising it expressly includes the operation
of free will.

In the first place, the final end is not some
benefit accruing to the Creator of which He
stands in need. God is the object of external
praise and glory. He chooses to receive it,
however, because it implies His bounteousness,
His spontaneity in giving of His treasure.

Nor yet is there a mechanism absorbing the various parts of creation. Wherever there is a rational creature there is an interplay of necessary and contingent causes. Nay, whatever of mechanism there is in the universe, it is intended to be at the service of the rational creation; and the right use of it is one of the ways in which man renders formal praise to the Creator. Thus the plan supposes that some intermediate ends should be brought about by contingent causes and some by necessary causes. "God moves the will of man like a universal power, moving the will to its universal object, namely that which is good. Without this universal motion man could not will anything. Yet man, by his reason, determines himself to will this or that, something which may be either a real good or only an apparent good. And sometimes, too, God moves men in a special way to will some definite good. This is the case when He moves them by grace." *

There has ever been a tendency in certain schools to look upon this action of God moving the will as something mechanical, and savouring of determinism. This comes about through an

---

* *Summa*, 1a. 2ae, quix, a. vi., ad. 3m.

abuse of analogy. The divine strength does not come from ourselves. It comes from God who is transcendent. But the transcendent God is also immanent. The power and particular movement which He gives to our wills, therefore, is not mechanical and superimposed from without, but vital and communicated from within. The God who is the Life of life is the energising principle of the action.

The analogy of a carpenter using a saw is good in so far as it represents God as distinct from ourselves, and keeps us from forming a pantheistic conception of Him. But it is inadequate. It might be supplemented by the analogy of a plant and its root. The root gives an impulse to the plant. This impulse, however, does not sterilise the proper action of the branches and leaves, but rather quickens it. So also the action of the will of God on the will of man does not destroy man's liberty, but rather promotes and ensures it as part of the divine plan.

Thus Christian finalism is the very antithesis of the doctrine of man's self-perfectibility. The whole meaning of Alpha and Omega is that man realises himself most by depending absolutely on God. Man is dependent on God for his beginning, for his continuation, and for his end. If he chooses his own method of perfecting himself, following only such goodness as attracts his sensual appetites, he will most assuredly not attain to independence. If he does not depend on God willingly as a vessel of mercy, he will have to depend upon Him unwillingly as a victim of justice. The general plan provides for these alternatives. Whether, therefore, a man freely turns to God, or whether he freely turns away from Him, the divine plan is realised. The sinner in hell shows forth the glory of God, manifesting His justice. The glory of formal praise is willed by God only conditionally, not absolutely. " I call heaven and earth to witness this day, that I have set before you life and death, blessing and cursing. Choose therefore life." *

Thus Christian finalism may be summed up in the beautiful words of Lactantius:

" The world was made that we might be born. We were born that we might know God. We know Him that we may worship

* *Deut.* xxx., 19.

Him. We worship Him that we may earn immortality. We are rewarded with immortality that, being made like unto the angels, we may serve our Father and Lord for ever, and be the eternal kingdom of God." *

* *Instit.* vii., 8.

CHAPTER VII

THE DIVINE FECUNDITY

SINCE everything in the philosophy of change is upside down, so we must examine the first cause last. We have seen the creative evolution in its flux, we have gathered that it can only be caught during flashes of intuition, we have understood that its direction is determined neither by mechanical forces nor intellectual motives, and we have tried to apprehend how the whole process could happen without any pre-conceived plan. We come now to examine the actual principle itself which is supposed to do all these things.

Of course we intend to use our intelligence in our inquiry. It is needful to make this remark because M. Bergson rather postulates that we shall not do so.

"Everything," he says, "is obscure in

the idea of creation if we think of *things*
which are created, and a *thing* which
creates, as we habitually do, as the understanding cannot help doing." *

That is just what the hatter said. "If you
knew Time as well as I do," said the Hatter,
"you wouldn't talk about wasting *it*. It's *him*."

"I don't know what you mean," said Alice.

"Of course you don't!" the Hatter said,
tossing his head contemptuously.†

If the new God Chronos is not intelligible
then it was silly to write a book describing him.
If we cannot make him intelligible we can at
least show where he is unintelligible.

Our first point of inquiry will be to see how
far the God Time involves a dualist or a monist
universe. In our first chapter ‡ we said that M.
Bergson professed to be a dualist. We now
venture to declare that, in spite of what he says,
and in spite of what his disciples may say, he is
a radical monist.

Monism § is a term invented by Wolff to

* *Creative Evolution*, p. 261.
† *Alice in Wonderland.*
‡ p. 2.
§ For a full treatment of this subject see: *Der Monismus und
seine philosophirahe Grucdlagen*, von Friedrich Klimke, S.J. Frei-
burg, Herder.

designate any philosophy which recognises in the whole sphere of existence only *one* (μόνος) kind of being. This kind of being may be either matter or spirit. If the one substance be regarded as matter then the monism is called materialist; if spirit, then it is called spiritualist. Spiritualist monism may be either intellectualist, voluntarist, or transcendental. A philosophy which teaches that there are two distinct kinds of being is known as dualist (δύο, two). If the monism is spiritualist it will include God and thus will be pantheistic. If it is materialist it will exclude God and thus will be atheistic.

At first sight there would seem to be in the system of M. Bergson two kinds of being, ascending life and descending matter. The ascending life is variously spoken of as " consciousness," " super-consciousness," " duration," " vital push," " choice," " freedom," " intuition," " will." It is never defined because it is seen only by intuition and so cannot be defined. From what we have observed, however, of its action and functions, we may describe it as a conscious vital push which sees intuitively and which wills according to the exigencies of creation.

Whatever else this force is or is not, it is original in the strictest sense of the word. However incoherent the statement may seem we are bound to say that in the system of M. Bergson this force creates itself. All at once, in the twinkling of an eye, with no sound of trumpet to herald its coming, nay, with no eye to twinkle upon it, it begins.

> "At a certain moment in certain points of space, a visible current has taken rise; this current of life, traversing the bodies it has organised one after another, passing from generation to generation, has become divided amongst species and distributed amongst individuals without losing anything of its force, rather intensifying in proportion to its advance." *

Again, this life which starts itself and intensifies itself, also bifurcates itself. The division into animal and vegetable lines, into the lines of instinct and reason are due to two causes which life bears within itself. As to the cause of these causes, well, it simply began at the given centre at which life began.

* *Creative Evolution*, p. 27.

" So of the way life breaks into individuals or species. It depends, we think, on two series of causes: the resistance life meets from inert matter, and the explosive force—due to an unstable balance of tendencies—which life bears within itself." *

" But the real and profound causes of division were those which life bore within its bosom. For life is tendency, and the essence of a tendency is to develop in the form of a sheaf, creating, by its very growth, divergent directions among which its impetus is divided." †

Here, be it noticed, we find matter already in existence and exercising its function of modifying life. But whence did the matter come? Did that start of itself from some given centre? In order to find out the genesis of matter we must recall the whole of the Bergsonian doctrine of time, space, intuition, and intellect. Then we shall see that this descending matter is but the inversion of ascending force.

First let us make a number of efforts at intuition. Each glimpse will give us a sight of the extra-spatial. Then as each glimpse fades

* *Creative Evolution*, p. 103.
† *Ibid.*, p. 104.

away the extra-spatial will be observed to degrade itself into spatiality. This will be all the more evident to us in proportion to the strain we put upon ourselves. Let us make ourselves self-conscious in the highest possible degree. Then we shall feel ourselves as it were, outside space and right in the middle of the fluid " now."

But then let us relax ourselves and fall back little by little. Then we shall feel that we are in the solid flesh after all, and that what was an indivisible flux has become a divisible extension.

"We have an extension of the self into recollections that are fixed and external to one another, in place of the tension it possessed as an indivisible active will." *

Our consciousness in this way shows us the direction of the movement. But it is not able to follow the whole course of the movement. Our intellect sees matter whilst our intuition sees life. And as our consciousness assumes now the form of intuition and now the form of intellect, we recognise that we hold two ends of a chain, though we do not succeed in seizing the intervening links.

* *Creative Evolution*, p. 219.

Philosophy, that is, intuition, has not yet become completely conscious of itself. But, since it is in a process of evolution, it may eventually come to see matter in its actual genesis. For the present, however, we may infer, by comparing our intuitional views with our intellectual views, that matter is but the inversion of life.

Physics has hitherto done its duty in pushing matter in the direction of spatiality. But metaphysics has been on the wrong track in simply treading in the footsteps of physics. It was a chimerical hope to expect to be able to go further in the same direction. It should have been recognised that the direction of intuition is the very opposite to that of intellect. The task of metaphysics should be "to remount the incline which physics descends, to bring back matter to its origins, and to build up progressively a cosmology which would be, so to speak, a reversed psychology. All that which seems *positive* to the physicist and to the geometrician would become from this new point of view, an interruption or inversion of the true positivity, which have to be defined in psychological terms." *

* *Creative Evolution*, p. 219.

Now if matter is but the inversion of spirit, if metaphysics is but the inversion of physics, and cosmology and psychology, then obviously there is but one radical kind of being. M. Bergson's observations are shrewd enough to show him the great difference between body and spirit. On the surface then he is a dualist. But he has to make this doctrine square with the doctrine of change. He has to account for the origin of that which is inert. So he makes matter the inversion of life. He begins as a dualist but ends as a monist.

Doubtless this idea of matter being but the inversion of life will not commend itself as being clear and coherent in itself. Indeed M. Bergson warns us that here we are entering the most obscure regions of metaphysics. Let us decline, however, to be hoodwinked. If M. Bergson is going to take us from the known to the unknown he must satisfy us as to the stepping-stones. He must not ask us to step out on to soft ooze, or into the dark, presuming that it will be all right. Observe then a few of his nebulosities.

" This long analysis (i.e. of the ideas of order and disorder) was necessary to show

how the real can pass from tension to extension and from freedom to mechanical necessity by way of inversion. . . . We must now examine more closely the inversion whose consequences we have just described. What then is the principle that has only to let go its tension—we may say to *detend*—in order to *extend* the interruption of the cause here being equivalent to a reversal of the effect? For want of a better word we have to call it consciousness. But we do not mean the narrowed consciousness that functions in each of us. Our own consciousness is the consciousness of a certain living being, placed in a certain point of space; and though it does indeed move in the same direction as its principle, it is continually drawn the opposite way, obliged, though it goes forward, to look behind. This retrospective vision is, as we have shown, the natural function of the intellect, and consequently of distinct consciousness." *

This is one of the most luminous passages we can find. We venture to interpret it as follows. Consciousness stretches itself as far as possible. Then it lets go. Or again, first it concentrates

* *Creative Evolution*, p. 250.

M

itself on itself for a living active moment. Then it allows itself to be distracted. Thus the stretching or concentrating makes tension. The letting go or dissipation makes detension. When the detending has finished extension is the result. Consciousness detends in order to extend. But only life can stretch itself or concentrate itself. And since matter is found already extended we presume that it has arrived through the detension of life. Hence we see that matter has its origin in life. If that is not clear pray listen again.

" Is it extension in general that we are considering *in abstracto? Extension*, we said, appears only as a tension which has been interrupted. Or, are we considering the concrete reality that fills this extension? The order which reigns there, and which is manifested by the laws of nature, is an order which must be born of itself when the inverse order is suppressed; a detension of the will would produce precisely this suppression.

" Lastly, we find that the direction which this reality takes, suggests to us the idea of a thing unmaking itself; such, no doubt, is one of the essential characters of materiality. What conclusion are we to draw from all this, if not that the process by which this thing makes itself is directed in a contrary way to that of physical processes, and that it is therefore, by its very definition, immaterial?

"The vision we have of the material world is that of a weight which falls; no image drawn from matter, properly so called, will ever give us the idea of weight rising. . . . All our analyses show us, in life, an effort to remount the incline that matter descends. In that they reveal to us the possibility, the necessity even of a process the inverse of materiality, creative of matter by its interruption alone." *

For the present let us suspend our judgment as to the coherence of this idea of inversion. Let us suppose that the interruption of the stream of life creates matter. Let us grant that the words represent a validly logical process and not a mere jumble of ideas. Then the point we have undertaken to make is established. If matter is but the inversion of spirit then both are ultimately one and the same thing, and M. Bergson whilst nominally a dualist is radically a monist.

* *Creative Evolution*, pp. 258-259.

" Intellect and matter," he says, " have progressively adapted themselves one to the other in order to attain at last a common form. This adaptation has, moreover, been brought about quite naturally, *because it is the same inversion of the same movement which creates at once the intellectuality of mind and the materiality of things."* *

This unification of the universe turns M. Bergson into a poet. Listen to his dithyramb:

" Thus to the eyes of a philosophy that attempts to re-absorb intellect in intuition many difficulties vanish or become light. But such a doctrine does not only facilitate speculation ; it gives us also more power to act and to live. For, with it, we feel ourselves no longer isolated in humanity, humanity no longer seems isolated in the nature that it dominates. As the smallest grain of dust is bound up with our entire solar system, drawn along with it in that undivided movement of descent which is materiality itself, so all organised beings, from the humblest to the highest, from the first origins of life to the time in which we are, and in all places as in all times, do but

* *Creative Evolution*, p. 217.

evidence a single impulsion, the inverse of the movement of matter, and in itself indivisible. All the living hold together, and all yield to the same tremendous push." *

Next we may note the incoherence of this new notion of inversion. An original impulse first starts off. But how does it turn back upon itself? Whence does it derive a direction antagonistic to itself? How can the very contradiction of a force spring from that force? How can descent be produced by ascent? Granting, in a word, that the vital push has certain potentialities, whence does it derive the principle by which these potentialities are actuated? Until these questions are answered, the whole concept must be written off as fraught with inconsistency and self-contradition.

Or again, we may note a vicious circle in the process. In order that life may ascend it is supposed to require matter to enable it to do so. Its ascent is a march of conquest. Matter is wanted to provide life with problems, the solution of which constitutes creative evolution. But in order that matter may be thus placed at

* *Creative Evolution*, p. 285.

the service of life, life must first ascend and become inverted. The ladder is upstairs. How shall we get it down? Here is a lacuna in the philosophy of change. The polite thing is just to peep at it and then cover it over again with the abundance of flowers which M. Bergson provides for us.

We have already seen, in our study of finalism, that no evolution could possibly have been set in motion without some intelligent direction. But something more is required than mere aim. The arrow does not fly off to the target by reason of its own self-propulsion. Motion presupposes a motor. So also is it with this vital push. Who started it pushing? Who pressed the button for such a wonderful system of change-ringing?

Both the principle of identity and the principle of causality are here skipped over as if they did not matter. But they do matter. We must write them down again, else we may be beguiled from the path of common sense. A thing is what it is as long as it is what it is, and so long as it is what it is it is not something else. That means that amoebas do not of themselves change their essence and merge into monkeys. An amoeba is always an amoeba and a monkey is always a monkey. Further, every effect must have a cause. But every change is an effect. Therefore every change must have a cause.

Most especially are these principles applicable to the changes in creative evolution. Here invariably the changes are from something less to something greater. They involve the extremely active conditions of intuition and freedom. Their glory is that by them are created absolutely new forms, unforeseen and unforeseeable. Whence come all these potentialities and activities? What makes instinct develop so astonishingly in the line of bees? What makes intelligence appear rather in the line of man? What holds back the mollusc with its splendid eyesight from entering into competition with man?

Evidently these questions have troubled M. Bergson. He speaks of the " torturing problems " to which the idea of " nothing " gives rise. Eventually he dares to admit that there is some great Principle at the bottom of the universe.

" Whence comes it," he asks, " and how can it be understood, that anything exists?

Even here in the present work, when matter has been defined as a kind of descent, this descent as the interruption of a rise, this rise itself as a growth, when finally a principle of creation has been put at the base of things, the same question springs up: How—why does this principle exist rather than nothing?"*

The answer to this question would be simple enough if M. Bergson had not poisoned the wells of knowledge. By wilfully suppressing the concept of "being," and substituting the concept of "becoming," he has blinded himself to that most obvious and primary truth, that a thing is what it is as long as it is what it is, the truth known as the principle of identity. Consequently he has cut himself off from that being who is essentially being. He has no place for being which exists of itself in one eternal and unchanging present. Having burnt his boats he has destroyed his only chance of escape. Hence he is in this predicament: he must create a God according to his own image and likeness.

On the one hand he allows himself to speak of his God as "a centre from which worlds shoot

* *Creative Evolution*, pp. 290-291.

out like rockets in a fireworks display"; * but on the other hand he says that he " does not present this centre as a *thing*, but as a continuity of shooting out. God, thus defined, has nothing of the already made; He is unceasing life, action, freedom." †   In other words, his God is the God of change, not the unchangeable God; the God of time, not the God of eternity.

M. Bergson has a number of names for this God, each more or less descriptive.   First we may consider the great principle as time.   That would be all very well if we used the word as a metaphor.   Time, for instance, can heal a broken heart.   Time, enough of it, enables eels to get used to being skinned.   But putting metaphors aside, we cannot think of time as creating anything at all.   It is not even an active principle.   It is merely an effect, the measurement of motion.

Or again, we may consider the principle as duration (*la durée*).   If I have endured from my birth until now, again that is an effect, not a cause.   If the creative principle is to produce anything at all it must at least produce existence.

* *Creative Evolution*, p. 262.
† *Ibid.*, p. 262.

But duration presupposes existence. I must actually be in existence in order to continue in existence. To say that duration is the creative principle of existence is to say that the effect is the cause of the cause.

Then we may regard the principle as a vital push. But a push supposes a pusher. There can be no action without an agent. Action without an agent would be a very useful commodity in business. There is a fortune awaiting the man who will discover it. It will drive steam engines without steam, electrical engines without electricity. But where will you find it? It is as elusive as a snark. You may seek it with thimbles, with care, with smiles, with forks, with hope, and with soap, and even then every time you put your finger on it you will find it is not there. Why? Because self-creation is an incoherent idea. And if it cannot exist as a concept of the mind, *a fortiori* it cannot exist in the world of reality.

No one gives what he has not got. Therefore no one can give existence who does not already possess it. The very notion of creation postulates a Creator.

Let us, however, for the sake of argument,

grant that there is a pure becoming which creates the things which we see, ourselves included. Even then the ultimate question would be still unanswered, for pure becoming could never be a *first* cause. M. Bergson indeed admits and claims that the pure becoming possesses some perfections and is devoid of others. It is partly in actuality and partly in potentiality. Being possessed of this double quality it necessarily presupposes a pure actuality. An absolutely first cause must be one that is actuated to every possible perfection.

Here we are at the very foundation of philosophy. We must begin with axioms. We submit the following as self-evident.

A thing is perfect in so far as it is in actuality; it is imperfect, however, in so far as it is in potentiality.

An altogether pure actuality is altogether perfect.

A potentiality as such can never reduce itself to actuality, but it must be reduced to actuality by some active principle.

Every changeable being possesses actuality and potentiality.

Actuality is always prior to potentiality.

Wherefore, since becoming has some perfection, it is partly in actuality. And since it is devoid of some perfection, it is partly in potentiality. Now whence did it derive its actuality? Certainly not from its potentiality, for no potentiality can reduce itself to actuality. We must therefore have recourse to some ultimate active principle which is pure actuality.

Hence we are driven back from the God of change, as described by M. Bergson, to the God of a full and active eternity, as described by St. Thomas.

"Everything that has in its substance," writes the Angelic Doctor, "an admixture of potentiality, to the extent that it has potentiality is liable not to be: because what can be, can also not be. But God in Himself cannot not be, seeing that He is everlasting; therefore there is in God no potentiality.

"Although in order of time, that which is sometimes in potentiality, sometimes in actuality, is in potentiality before it is in actuality, yet, absolutely speaking, actuality is prior to potentiality, because potentiality does not bring itself into actuality, but is brought into actuality by something which is already in actuality. Everything therefore that is in any way in potentiality has something else prior to it. But God is the first being, and the first cause, and therefore has not in Himself any admixture of potentiality.

"Everything acts inasmuch as it is in actuality. Whatever then is not all actuality, does not act by its whole self, is not a prime agent; for it acts by participation in something else, not by its own essence. The prime agent then, which is God, has no admixture of potentiality, but is pure actuality.

"We see that there is that in the world which passes from potentiality to actuality. But it does not educe itself from potentiality to actuality, because what is in potentiality is not as yet, and therefore cannot act. Therefore there must be some other prior thing, whereby this thing may be brought out from potentiality to actuality. And again, if this further thing is going out from potentiality to actuality, there must be posited before it yet some other thing, whereby it may be reduced to actuality. But this process cannot go on for ever: therefore we must come to something that is only in actuality, and nowise in potentiality; and that we call God." *

Even then though we did grant that the principle of creative evolution were a pure becoming the problem would still remain as to how, why, when, and wherefore that becoming began to become.

The truth is that M. Bergson has reversed the dictates of common sense. He has made becoming prior to being; he has made potentiality superior to actuality; he has made nonbeing superior to being. Worked out to its ultimate absurdity, his philosophy implies that the first cause is non-being. Then where did we all come from? We simply grew.

Listen how M. Bergson avows all this:

" We said " he writes " there is *more* in a movement than in the successive positions attributed to the moving object, *more* in a becoming than in the forms passed through in turn, *more* in the evolution of form than in the forms assumed one after another." †

Thus becoming is more perfect than being, a

* *Contra Gentes*. Lib. I., Cap. XVI.
† *Creative Evolution*, p. 333.

mixture of potentiality and actuality more perfect than pure actuality.

But once again, no one can give what he has not got. A man can not do more than he is "up to." The imperfect cannot *of itself* roll out into the perfect. Hence self-perfectibility is seen to be not only a theological heresy, but also a metaphysical absurdity.

At this point we may ask why should M. Bergson, and with him the whole school of modernist philosophy, prefer a changeable and perfectible God to an unchangeable and all-perfect God. It is because they will not take the trouble to understand St. Thomas's doctrine. They will regard unchangeableness as a sort of petrifaction. They will not see in it the very fulness of activity. They, who are so ready to impute anthropomorphism to the orthodox, are themselves shut up in the crudest anthropomorphism. Seeing that the *anthropos* is always changing they are unable to rise to the concept of a *theos* which never changes. Their mistake is not that of thinking of God in human thought-forms. We all do that, nor can we think of God in any other way. Their mistake is in forgetting that their thought-forms are human, and in taking them to be adequate representations of the ultimate unspeakable reality.

Having pointed out the shortcomings of the God of time and change, it remains for us to give a more positive description of our own timeless and unchangeable God. He not only possesses life, and gives life to all living creatures, but He is life itself.

Our knowledge of God's life can only be obtained by inference of what we know of our own. Now we know of our own lives that they are imperfect. Every day we gain new experience. There is always something new for us to know and to enjoy. No morrow comes and finds us exactly in the same condition as we were yesterday. We are always in a state of transition from potentiality to actuality.

God, on the contrary, since He is absolutely perfect, is incapable of acquiring new perfections. His incapacity to change is due not to an exhaustion or want of activity, but to a complete fulness of activity. This activity indeed is so perfect and absolute that it admits of no potentiality whatever. Hence He is incapable of any transition from potentiality to actuality.

The life therefore which we attribute to God

is life of the most eminent kind, a kind wholly
different from ours, for it is all pure actuality.
Ours is only a participation of life, and so we
are said to possess life.   But God is all life, and
so we say that He *is* life.   No one gives it to
Him.   He is it from all eternity.

Moreover, He gives it to all who share in it.
He is the Life of all lives.   " Ye men of Athens
. . . God who made the world and all things
therein, He, being Lord of heaven and earth,
dwelleth not in temples made with hands, neither
is He served with men's hands as if He needed
anything; seeing it is He who giveth to all life,
and breath, and all things." *

Nor is the life of God a sort of fiery volcano,
not a huge disordered sphere of activity with a
continuity of shooting out.   Divine life is
activity of the highest order.   We give it the
nearest description possible when we say that it
is a life of perfect wisdom.

Again, even the wisdom which we attribute to
God is known only by the analogy of human
wisdom.   Human wisdom is that mental activity
which peers into both speculative and practical
truth, and ordains things to their proper end.

* *Acts* xvii., 22 *et seq.*

N

This is undoubtedly the supreme attribute of God. It is the highest form of spirit life that we can imagine. When we speak of God as the Being, that does not express to us His vital activity. When we speak of Him as the Life, that does not express to us the more interesting attributes of knowledge and love. But when we speak of Him as the Wisdom, then we express His life of intelligence and love, and we see how this intelligence and love acts both within and without, inwardly understanding and loving the Divine Essence, outwardly understanding and loving all creation.

Thus it is by His wisdom that God knows all possible truth, and loves all possible good. It is by His wisdom that He forms a due estimate of the value of all things in reference to His final plan. It is by His wisdom that He is able to economise and order all things in accord with this plan. Hence wisdom expresses the sum total of God's activities, that full perfection of life, so perfect as to admit of no further perfection.

Moreover, this activity of divine intellect and will is no cold intellectualism or uninterested volitionalism. It is an activity which constitutes an infinite happiness and glory.

Happiness is the satisfaction and restfulness in the fruition of some good known and loved. But God both knows and loves the most perfect goodness and beauty. He is Himself the exemplar and source of all possible goodness and beauty. But He knows Himself. Such knowledge can only prompt the most perfect love. Such love can only make the most perfect rapture and happiness.

This divine activity, too, produces the greatest possible splendour. The divine intelligence and love are aglow with the riches of truth and goodness. We all know the brightness of a household where a happy child is playing about. Happiness sheds brightness everywhere and always. Every little ray of brightness which is shed by a happy creature is an indication of the glory which emanates from the divine blessedness. If God's happiness is supreme so also must His splendour be supreme. Well may St. Timothy speak of " the glory of the blessed God." *

This fact of God deriving His happiness and splendour from His own intrinsic wealth serves again to show up the fallacy of the modern

*1 *Tim.* i., 11.

doctrine of man's self-perfectibility. If one thing is obvious in the present rush and tear of society it is that a man can never be satisfied with his own intrinsic wealth. He must always be seeking happiness from without. Every improvement in his well-being is due to some educative influence from without, and if the series of causes which contribute to man's happiness be traced to their ultimate source, they will be found to lead to that cause which is uncaused, the God whose happiness and splendour is supreme, the wisdom which has no needs within itself, but which is the satisfaction of all needs outside itself.

Naturally we pay more attention to the divine fecundity which is manifested in creation than to that which is active within the bosom of God Himself. Yet, after all, the inner fecundity of God is the most important of all mysteries. It has a practical bearing on our own lives. If only we could realise a little more the intrinsic beauties of the Godhead, we should appreciate more the divine condescension in creating an outer world to share in the divine happiness. The outward fecundity of God takes on a much greater significance when considered together with the inward fecundity of God, the mystery of the Blessed Trinity.

We do not pretend that we can explain either the mystery without or the mystery within. A mystery is a truth which is partly revealed and partly concealed. But what we do say is that if we take these mysteries as we know them, that is, in so far as they are revealed to our understanding, even then, they are far more intelligible than the Bergsonian fireworks.

Let us first try to apprehend something of the richness, fulness, and consistency of the inner fecundity of the divine life.

To begin with, God is a pure and infinite actuality. In this He is essentially different from all His creatures. Consequently His internal productivity will be quite different from that which we observe in creatures. It is not a reproduction of the divine nature as the formation of a new man is the reproduction of a human nature. We are forbidden to say that there can be three Gods.

Nor yet is the inner fecundity a production of organisms whereby the divine life may develop and extend itself. It is wholly within, wholly immanent. It is an energy which is expressed in distinct subjects, yet all within the one divine nature.   What can these subjects be?

Once again we have recourse to human analogies.   We ask ourselves what are the highest forms of activity that we know. They are intelligence and will.   And the subject in which intelligence and will are united is a personality. How shall we describe these personalities?

We have seen that the attribute of wisdom is the most adequate description of the divine life that we can think of.   This term also indicates the kind of fecundity.   Wisdom is at once the most perfect knowledge of the most perfect truth and the most perfect love of the most perfect good.   The divine fecundity therefore issues as acts of the divine intellect and the divine will. The results of these acts must express and complete the divine knowledge and volition. As finished products they are the most perfect outcome of the divine wisdom. Each of them is a complete actuality, unmixed with the slightest trace of any potentiality.   If this were not so they would not be complete. They would still be capable of additional perfection.

But the perfect wisdom of God consists of two activities, namely knowledge and volition.

As the outcome of the divine fecundity, therefore, there will be two personalities, one issuing as the divine intelligence, the other as the divine love.   But intelligence and love in God are not independent of each other.   God neither understands without loving nor loves without understanding.   Knowledge is the way to love.   Even in the divine fecundity nothing can be loved that is not already known.   Hence the knowledge, which is the term of the divine understanding, is a knowledge which breathes forth love.   To the personality which is the principle of the divine fecundity there is given the appropriate name of Father; to that which is the offspring by way of understanding, the name of Son; and to that which is the offspring by way of a double breathing out of love, the name of Holy Ghost.

Taken at its lowest estimate this account of the inner fecundity of God is a magnificent working hypothesis.   It is fraught with none of the puerilities of the Bergsonian half-made centre which is a continuity of shooting-out. Although the union of three persons in one nature is a truth transcending human reason it does not do violence to human reason in the way that the Bergsonian speculations do.   And when the theory is read in the light of the inspired word it becomes much more than a reasonable working hypothesis. It becomes a certitude of a very high order.

See, for instance, how the title Wisdom is appropriated to the Son because He is the reflection of the Father. Notice how the title *Logos* of the Greek Testament harmonises with the *Verbum* of the scholastics. Both concepts were derived from widely different sources, yet both are most aptly used to express the supreme, initial, eternal and final judgment of the Godhead. So, too, with the Holy Spirit. He is said to proceed as the " Gift " or " Pledge " of love. And if love in human beings is essentially an act of the will, and not passion or feeling, much more so is it in God. Just as knowledge tends towards expression, so love tends towards effusion.

The difficulty of forming a mental picture of all this productivity is due to our experience of ourselves. When we produce things it is because we want them. In God there is no want. The real basis of the divine fecundity is not a need to produce something. It is not the need of further perfection. It is the very fulness of divine life. By the light of reason we could never have guessed that this fecundity would issue in two divine persons. But after the revelation has been received, we can see how very reasonable it is.

So, too, is it with the mystery of creation. Without the revelation we should be in the same boat with M. Bergson, tortured with the problem as to why anything should be. But, knowing the fulness and the richness of the divine fecundity, we have no difficulty in looking to God's Will as the reason for the existence of creation.

Since God is the only necessary being, the only perfect and full actuality, all other beings must owe their existence to Him. Nor are they made out of His substance. His perfect actuality, simplicity and unchangeableness excludes that supposition. They must, therefore, be made out of nothing. And when in this context, we use the word " nothing " we do not mean " something." The nought is not a sort of half-defined blue jelly out of which things were made. It is merely the term from which things begin to be. The word " nothing " simply means not-being.

Our apology for making such crude remarks is that M. Bergson, in his characteristic way, juggles with the word "nothing," endeavouring to show that, through misuse of the word, the problem of existence is but a pseudo-problem. Hitherto, he says, man has had a false idea of the nought. If only we could get rid of the false idea of the nothingness, then the problem as to why anything should exist would vanish.

Through twenty-six highly decorative pages * of literature M. Bergson labours to show up this false idea of nothingness. The idea of "nothing" is either an *image*, or a *positive* idea, or a *negative* idea. Quite easily he disposes of the first two suppositions, and incidentally paints a word-picture of "nothing" which is worthy of a frame and a place in a post-impressionist gallery. We quite agree with him in his contention that we can neither form an image of "nothing," nor identify it with "something."

We disagree with him, however, when he contends that we cannot have even a negative idea of "nothing."

"To sum up," he says, "for a mind which

* *Creative Evolution*, pp. 288-314.

should follow purely and simply the thread of experience, there would be no void, no nought, even relative or partial, *no possible negation.*   Such a mind would see facts succeed facts, states succeed states, things succeed things.   What it would note at each moment would be things existing, states appearing, events happening.   It would live in the actual, and, if it were capable of judging, it would never affirm anything except the existence of the present." *

Here we must answer with a distinction.   We grant that an absolute nought cannot be affirmed. We deny that an absolute nought cannot be thought.   The absolute nought is a being of the mind (*ens rationis*), not being amongst things which appear and happen (*ens reale*).   Our whole contention throughout these studies has been that the real is that which exists whether the mind knows about it or not.   So, too, the unreal is that which does not exist, notwithstanding whether the mind thinks about it or not.   Hence we can think of the nought, without the nought having any objective reality.   The

* *Creative Evolution*, p. 310.

absolute nought is a pure figment of the mind.

With this distinction before him let the reader go through M. Bergson's last statement and notice the logical fallacy uttered in every word. The fallacy is known as the illicit transit from the ontological to the logical order. Thus the author asks us to follow the thread of concrete experience; to observe that facts succeed facts, states succeed states, and things succeed things; to notice that there is no "nought" in the realm of reality; and then to jump to the conclusion that there can be no "nought" in the realm of abstractions. Of course this logical fallacy arises from the previous psychological fallacy of confusing abstract thought with concrete feeling.

Once again St. Thomas has anticipated the difficulty and answered it. Discussing the question as to whether truth is commensurate and identical with being, he thus formulates his objection:

"That which extends to being and non-being is not identical and commensurate with being. But truth extends to being and non-being; for both statements are equally true, that what is is, and what is not is not. Therefore, truth and being are not identical and commensurate."

To this difficulty he replies as follows:

"Non-being has not got that in itself whereby it may be recognised. Still it may be recognised in so far as the intellect renders it knowable. Hence truth is only based on non-being in so far as non-being is a being of the reason, that is in so far as it is apprehended by the reason." *

Then if we turn to the *Contra Gentes* we shall find passages which might have been expressly written to refute the philosophy of change.

"Hence appears the futility of arguments against creation drawn from the nature of movement or change—as that creation must be in some subject, or that not-being must be transmuted into being; for creation is not a change but is the mere dependence of created being on the principle by which

---

* *Summa*, p. 1, qu. xvi., a. 3., ad 2m. The Latin is more apt than English for manipulating the verb "to be." *Id quod extendit ad ens, et non ens, non convertitur cum ente : sed verum se extendit ad ens et non ens : nam verum est, quod est esse, et quod non est non esse : ergo verum et ens non convertunutr.*

it is set up, and so comes under the category of *relation* : hence the subject of creation may very well be said to be the thing created. Nevertheless, creation is spoken of as a " change " according to our mode of conceiving it, inasmuch as our understanding takes one and the same thing to be now non-existent and afterwards existing." *

So St. Thomas was quite alive to the tendency of the human mind to regard " nothing " as " something." But, on the other hand, he was not such a muddled thinker as to be beguiled into confusing the " nought " of thought with the " nought " of reality. The " nought " of thought must of necessity be retained to designate the non-being from which, through the activity of the all-active Creator, creation began to be.

Thus the last fallacy of the philosophy of change is seen to spring from the same source as the first and all intervening ones, namely, the denial of the validity of human intelligence. If we maim the natural instrument of thought, then

* *Contra Gentes*, Lib. II. Cap. XVIII. See also *Cap. XIX.*

we must not be surprised if we see things upside down or inside out. If we destroy intelligence, the faculty of truth, then we must not expect to enjoy that repose and satisfaction which comes only of the contemplation of truth.

But, on the other hand, if we resolutely determine that we will not prostitute our reason, but that we will keep it enthroned as the ruler of life, then we may hope to make the best of life.

Through intuitive reason we can see the first principles of knowledge, that things are what they normally appear to be, that every effect must have a cause, and that no effect is greater than its cause.

Through discursive reason we can argue back to the uncaused cause of all causes, to the pure actuality whence comes all participated actuality, to that infinitely fecund Life which is the Life of life. Does M. Bergson tell us that by turning away from intelligence and turning to animal instinct we shall get into touch with life? Pooh! Does he tell us that by retracing the steps which reason has laboriously cut out for us we shall attain to the highest life? Pooh! Pooh! It might take us to the life of time. But that is not what we happen to want. We want the life of eternity, the perfect possession, wholly and all at once, of life without end. And that happens to consist of intellectual knowledge, the knowledge of the only true God and of Jesus Christ whom He has sent.

NOTE.—Acknowledgment is made to the editor of the *Catholic World* for kind permission to reproduce copy.

THE END

THE NORTHUMBERLAND PRESS, THORNTON STREET, NEWCASTLE-UPON-TYNE